I0559521

IS MANI FESTING
BULLSHIT?
PART 2 - **THE LIMIT IS YOU**

CINDY WITTEMAN
RENEE VARDOUNIOTIS | SONNY VON CLEVELAND | NORMA CAVAZOS | KYSTALORE CREWS

TABLE OF CONTENTS

INTRODUCTION

I am absolutely thrilled to share with you part two of the International Best-Selling Book, "Is Manifesting Bullshit?". This book holds a very special place in my heart, and I can't wait for you to dive into the incredible journeys within its pages.

In this edition, you'll meet some truly inspiring individuals who have manifested the lives of their dreams. These are not just tales of success but deeply personal stories filled with struggle, diversity, pain, abuse, and even overwhelming trauma. As you read, you'll walk alongside them through their darkest times and witness how they found the strength to rise above it all.

Each author in this book faced immense challenges and unimaginable stress. Yet, they discovered a remarkable inner power that propelled them to greatness. Their stories are raw and real, a testament to the resilience of the human spirit. What I find most inspiring is how they didn't stop at their own success; they turned their experiences into a source of strength to help others.

These authors have taken their unique life challenges and harnessed that inner power to reach out and lift others from the darkness. They show us that no matter how tough life gets, there is always a way to find the light within and use it to create a positive impact on the world.

As you turn the pages, you'll feel their pain, their triumphs, and the incredible journeys that led them to where they are now. Their stories will move you, inspire you, and perhaps even challenge you to look within yourself for that same power.

But that's not all. Get ready to learn the tips and tricks discovered by the authors throughout their journeys. Find practical ways to apply all they have learned to your own life so you can manifest the life you have been dreaming of. These insights are not just inspiring; they are actionable, offering you a roadmap to harness your own potential and transform your dreams into reality.

So, get ready for an emotional and uplifting experience. Let these stories remind you of the boundless potential that lies within each of us and inspire you to harness your own inner power.

Cindy Witteman

Founder and CEO of Driving Single Parents Inc. CF Views LLC

https://www.linkedin.com/in/cindy-witteman-a48851253
https://www.facebook.com/cindy.witt.902
https://www.instagram.com/cindy.witteman/
https://drivingsingleparents.org/
https://cfviews.com/little-give-tv-show-1

Cindy Witteman is a passionate and purpose-driven leader based in San Antonio, Texas. As the Founder and Editor-in-Chief of FORCE Magazine, a business owner, and a 4x best-selling author, Cindy is committed to creating positive change and telling impactful stories. Her work has earned her the 2023 International Impact Book Award and the Trailblazer Award, as well as the 2024 International Impact Book Award for her solo book, "Beyond the Smile".

Cindy also hosts the "Little Give" TV Show and the "Is Manifesting Bullshit" podcast, where she shares insights and inspires transformation. An entrepreneur, action mastery coach, speaker, and beekeeper, Cindy wears many hats, each allowing her to connect with people in meaningful ways.

Family is at the core of Cindy's life. She cherishes time with her blended family of six children, two grandsons, and two granddaughters. Whether exploring new destinations or enjoying quiet moments together, these experiences are deeply valued.

In 2017, Cindy founded Driving Single Parents Inc., a nonprofit dedicated to helping single parents regain their independence. Through this organization, Cindy and her team have provided reliable vehicles to single-parent families, helping them overcome challenges and achieve their dreams.

Cindy is dedicated to spreading hope and making a difference, one little give at a time. For more about her work, visit DrivingSingleParents.org, tune in to the "Little Give" TV Show at LittleGive.com, or explore her other projects at CFViews.com.

Are You Willing to See It Differently?

By Cindy Witteman

What is manifesting, and why do so many people use that term? Manifesting might seem like another buzzword. You're right; the term has indeed become popular. In a world where everyone is looking for a quick fix to their problems, it's easy to fall for the hype. However, manifesting is more than just wishful thinking. In this section, I will share a practical guide to living a life that even surprises you!

Before I Share My Tips for Manifesting the Life of Your Dreams

Before I dive into sharing my tips for manifesting the life of your dreams, I want to take a moment to share a bit of my story, especially if this is your first time hearing about my journey.

My Love for Manifesting

My passion for manifesting didn't stem from a place of abundance or ease; it was born out of sheer desperation. If you've read my previous books, you already know that my journey has been anything but smooth. Growing up, I watched my mom and extended family struggle financially.

In an attempt to escape the financial struggles I faced while living with my mom, I got married at a very young age, hoping it would lead to my own happily ever after. But life had other plans. After many years of marriage, I found myself escaping a domestic violence situation and becoming a single mom—a reality I had always vowed wouldn't be the case for me and my daughters. It was in this challenging time that my true self-development journey began.

Listening to the audiobook *Think and Grow Rich* marked a turning point for me. It opened my eyes to the power of gratitude and positive thinking, completely transforming how I viewed my circumstances and my future. One day, I reached my breaking point and thought, "Enough is enough." I decided to give manifesting a try because, honestly, what did I have to lose? At that point, I was already living my worst-case scenario—struggling to make ends meet as a single mom, living paycheck to paycheck, and even selling plasma just to get by. It seemed like that was all life had in store for me, but deep down, I knew there had to be more.

Spending time with my dad, who had financial stability, showed me that there was another way. I began asking people how they managed to achieve that kind of security, and I eventually realized that to change my circumstances, I needed a solid job and the knowledge to use money as a tool.

As I navigated through those tough times and finally found stability, I took a leap of faith and leaned into self-belief. That leap led me to found the nonprofit Driving Single Parents Inc., with a mission to help other single parents by providing reliable family vehicles to get them back on the road and back on their feet.

When I first launched the nonprofit, I was eager to share its mission with anyone who would listen. But I quickly discovered a deep, crippling fear of public speaking that hit me like a ton of bricks whenever I was asked to speak—whether on camera or in front of a crowd. Realizing how much this fear was holding me back, I promised myself that I would face it head-on. I decided to embrace every speaking opportunity that came my way and just do it scared until I finally broke free from that self-limiting belief. Very shortly after, I was offered the opportunity to co-author a book titled *Shattering the Stigma of Single Motherhood*, before I knew it, book deal number two was offered, and I accepted.

Manifesting My Company

Now that you're up to speed, let me share one of my favorite manifesting success stories. When I was offered the opportunity to write my second book, *How to Overcome Self-Sabotage*, I was thrilled but also a bit anxious. I wondered, "Where am I going to sell this book? It doesn't really fit with what I'm currently doing or with Single Parents in Need or any of my other ventures."

My initial idea was to create a landing page to drive traffic and make sales. I even considered diving into a new business, though I had no idea what it would focus on or what I'd offer. All I had at that point was my first book, *Shattering the Stigma of Single Motherhood*. But deep down, I knew I wanted to start something new, and this was just the beginning of my journey.

I suddenly remembered that I'd previously named my business CF Views, a few years back when I had an idea for a DIY party event service. I'd even purchased a URL and sketched out logos, but then COVID hit, and I put the idea on hold. Despite the uncertainty, I decided to push forward, believing that things would eventually come together—just like when I launched my nonprofit with nothing but an idea and a desire to give back. I began building the website, featuring my two books, and brainstorming ways to generate income for this new venture.

This whole experience was a perfect example of how something I thought was a lost cause was actually developing in the background all along. The fact that I had secured a five-year plan for CFViews.com years before proved that this idea was quietly growing in my mind, even when I thought I had abandoned it.

It reminds me of Ed Mylett's book *The Power of One More*, where he describes a piñata at a kids' party. Everyone takes a swing at it, and it seems like nothing is happening until finally, someone cracks it open, and the candy spills out. That's how CF Views felt. Even when I thought I had let go of the idea, my mind was still working on it, waiting for the right moment to bring it back to life. Everything was in place, ready for me to act, and when the time was right, it all fell into place beautifully. You never know when what you've been working on behind the scenes will suddenly make perfect sense.

So, I began journaling and dreaming about what CF Views could become. Almost immediately, I realized that people had been approaching me for coaching to help them build their own success stories. If I was already helping others, why not make it a formal part of my business? I decided to pursue certification as a life and confidence coach, and after completing the course, I added coaching services to my website.

When I finished that second book *How to Overcome Self-Sabotage* and added it to my site, I focused on how to help others create their own success stories. Out of the blue, I was offered the opportunity to host a TV show. I could name it, develop its mission, pick my guests, and shape it my way. Remembering my commitment to start and embrace fear, I said yes to hosting *Little Give with Cindy*. The show highlights ordinary people doing extraordinary things and features nonprofits from around the world.

Suddenly, my website was filled with new offerings, including my solo book *Beyond the Smile*. I began speaking at engagements, appeared on podcasts, and was featured in magazines. My "In the Media" tab showcased my expanding business and services.

After achieving four international best-selling books, hosting a TV show, launching a podcast, and receiving numerous awards, someone asked me, "What's next for you?" At first, I thought, "Seriously? Now I need to come up with even more?" For three nights, just before bed, I wrote down the question, "What's next for you?" This prompted me to reflect deeply. Was I truly finished? What was next?

On the third night, I dreamt about starting my own magazine titled *FORCE—to Be Reckoned With*. It felt like the perfect next step. I woke up, sketched out the idea, and called my publicist at She Rises Studios. They were excited and said, "Yes, we can help you with that." Soon after, *FORCE* magazine was launched in 13 countries and became a best-seller, adding yet another dimension to the website that once had no clear direction.

It's incredible how something that seemed uncertain can evolve into something extraordinary. You never know when your behind-the-scenes efforts will come together and make perfect sense. The point of the story is to share with all of you that if you build it, they will come. You truly have to lean into your why, focus less on how opportunities will come, and capitalize on them to build the life of your dreams. Don't get caught up in the "How will I do this?" and "How will I do that?" and let fear or your inability to see the full vision in the moment stop you. Just lean in and embrace your why, and that will help you propel to the next level in ways you never dreamed of.

Think of it this way—do you wait for every traffic light to turn green before you get in the car and start driving? Of course not. You get in, start driving, and figure things out as you go. Along the way, you might have to yield, stop at a few red lights, or even avoid an accident, but you always find a way to reach your destination, even if it takes longer than you planned. Life works the same way—once you know where you want to go, you can use the tools and skills you have to navigate the best route as you move forward.

Manifesting is like a personal journey where you focus your thoughts and energy to bring something you deeply desire into reality. When I talk about desire, I am not necessarily talking about money, fancy homes, or cars. I am talking about fulfillment. Not just surface-level—deep fulfillment is where the magic is.

Manifestation is more than just a buzzword or wishful thinking—it's a tool for creating real change in your life. But for it to truly work, it requires both intention, consistent action, being open to opportunities, and deep self-reflection. Before diving into manifesting your desires, it's important to pause and ask yourself: Why do I want this? Are my desires coming from a place of fear, lack, or comparison to others? Or are they rooted in a genuine need for growth, fulfillment, and alignment with my true self? Without this self-awareness, manifestation can feel empty and might only serve temporary wants without addressing the deeper layers.

In the end, manifestation isn't just about visualizing a better life. It's about understanding your motivations, accepting challenges as part of your path, and aligning your energy with what you truly want. When approached with clarity and intention, manifestation becomes a powerful tool for creating meaningful change.

I can already hear your next question bubbling up inside: "This sounds wonderful, amazing, even life-changing... but HOW the heck do I actually do it? Is it even possible for me?" Maybe you're thinking, "Cindy must just be lucky or special." Well, it's a good thing you picked up this book, because by the time you finish, you'll have practical ways to apply manifestation to your own life, and you'll see that it *is* possible for you too—luck had nothing to do with it. Once you realize that the only limit is YOU, life gets so much easier. So, get ready to take notes and learn all the tips and tricks you'll need to create the incredible life you once thought was only for "others."

Let's first break down some myths.

If You Think It, It Will Happen

This idea is completely off base. To achieve what you truly want, start by clearly defining your goals. It's essential to understand exactly what you're aiming for and set a specific target. Once you have this clarity, break it down into daily, actionable steps. These small, manageable tasks will keep you moving forward and make the process less overwhelming.

One method I highly recommend is the "Think in Ink" technique. This involves writing down your goals and the specific actions you need to take to reach them. The power of this method lies in how it makes your goals tangible and actionable. When you put your thoughts into writing, you create a concrete plan that helps you stay focused and committed.

Regularly reviewing and updating your written plan allows you to track your progress and make necessary adjustments. This ongoing process keeps your goals at the forefront of your mind and helps you stay motivated. By turning your dreams into a detailed, written roadmap, you transform abstract aspirations into clear, achievable objectives. This approach not only guides you but also boosts your confidence as you see yourself making steady progress toward your ultimate goal.

Money Would Solve All of My Problems

Let me tell you, money isn't everything. It's easy to think that if you just had enough money, all your problems would disappear. But in reality, chasing money can sometimes hold you back more than it helps. Take lottery winners, for example. You'd think that winning the lottery would be the answer to all their problems, but studies show a different story. Many lottery winners end up facing serious financial troubles and personal issues after their big win. In fact, according to the National

Endowment for Financial Education, about 70% of people who suddenly receive a large sum of money, whether through an inheritance, legal settlement, or lottery winnings, end up broke within a few years. Even more startling, research from the University of Kentucky found that lottery winners are more likely to declare bankruptcy within three to five years than the average American.

So, why does sudden wealth often lead to even more problems? There are a few reasons. First, many people who suddenly come into money simply aren't prepared to handle it. Without a solid understanding of financial literacy, it's easy to make poor investment choices, fall for scams, or overspend on luxury items. The excitement of newfound wealth can quickly spiral into a spending spree, leading to lifestyle inflation where expenses skyrocket with no sustainable plan to maintain them. It's not just the financial side, either—there's also the pressure that comes from friends and family who might expect a piece of the pie. This can strain relationships and create stress as you navigate who to help and how much to give.

On top of that, the emotional and psychological toll of managing a sudden influx of money can be overwhelming. The responsibility and expectations that come with wealth can trigger anxiety, depression, and other mental health challenges. Trust issues often arise, too, as you might start questioning the motives of those around you, which can lead to isolation and difficulty maintaining genuine relationships. And when stress levels rise, some people turn to unhealthy coping mechanisms, like substance abuse. The *Journal of Gambling Studies* even reported that lottery winners are more prone to depression and anxiety, largely due to the pressures and drastic lifestyle changes that come with sudden wealth.

All of this goes to show that while money can bring temporary relief and open doors to new opportunities, it's not a magic solution to life's problems. In fact, it can sometimes make things even more complicated.

A Little Less Talk and a Lot More Action

Now that we've busted some of the myths, let's dive into some actionable steps that can springboard you towards true happiness.

First, set a clear intention. Think about something you truly want to achieve, whether it's a new project or a personal goal. Next, visualize it. Spend time each day imagining that you've already reached this goal—envision every detail, like how it feels, what you see, and the joy it brings you. Then, believe in it. Trust that this goal is more than just a dream; it's a real possibility. Feel confident that it will come to you in due time. After that, take action. Begin with small steps toward this goal—whether it's brainstorming ideas, thinking in ink, meeting new people, or acquiring skills that align with your vision. Finally, stay positive. Maintain a positive attitude. Even when obstacles arise, keep your focus on the end goal and remain hopeful.

By keeping your thoughts, emotions, and actions aligned with what you desire, you can create the reality you envision.

One of the most powerful tools you have at your disposal is gratitude. It's easy to get caught up in the hustle and overlook the true gifts that are right in front of us. The roof over your head might seem ordinary to you, but it's the dream of someone who's homeless. That job you might not love? It's the goal of someone who's unemployed. It all comes down to perspective.

In today's fast-paced world, we often get swept up in the pursuit of more—more success, more money, more recognition. This constant chase can blind us to the simple yet profound blessings we already have. Social media only fuels this fire, as it often makes it look like everyone else is living their best life, leaving us feeling like we're falling behind. But when we stop to practice gratitude, we start to see things differently.

Research backs this up. Studies show that regularly practicing gratitude can have a profound impact on your well-being. For instance, psychologists Dr. Robert Emmons and Dr. Michael McCullough found that people who keep a gratitude journal experience fewer physical symptoms, feel better about their lives, and are more optimistic about the future. Gratitude doesn't just make you feel better—it makes you more resilient, helping to ward off feelings of depression and anxiety by shifting your focus from what you lack to what you have.

Gratitude also strengthens your relationships. When you express appreciation for others, you build trust and deepen your connections with them. This creates a positive cycle: The more you recognize and appreciate the kindness of others, the more likely they are to continue those supportive behaviors.

So how can you bring more gratitude into your life? Start by keeping a gratitude journal where you write down three things you're thankful for each day. This simple habit can help shift your focus from what's wrong to what's right in your life. Take time to express your thanks to the people around you—whether it's a handwritten note, a phone call, or just a simple "thank you." Practicing mindfulness through meditation or deep breathing can also help you stay present and appreciate the moment. When negative thoughts creep in, try to reframe them by focusing on what you have rather than what's missing. And don't forget to give back—performing acts of kindness can boost your own sense of gratitude while helping others.

By making gratitude a part of your daily routine, you can stop chasing external validation and start finding happiness in the simple, often overlooked blessings that surround you. It's all about shifting your perspective, recognizing the abundance in your life, and fostering a deep sense of contentment and joy.

Speaking of perspective, did you know that how you perceive the world is largely within your control? When things go wrong, you have a choice in how you let them affect you. Emotions are natural, but we often dwell in negative feelings for too long, leaving us stuck. However, when you actively shape your perspective, you can make a big difference in how you experience life.

Your perception of events shapes your reality more than the events themselves. This concept is a cornerstone of cognitive-behavioral therapy (CBT), which teaches that our thoughts about a situation influence our feelings and behaviors. By changing how we think, we can change how we feel and act. While you can't always control what happens to you, you can control how you respond.

Imagine being stuck in traffic, late for an important meeting. You could see it as a disaster, leading to stress and frustration. Or, you could view it as an opportunity to practice patience, listen to a favorite podcast, or plan your day. The situation doesn't change, but your perspective determines your experience.

If you're not open to seeing things differently, this book might not be for you. If you believe life just happens to you and everything is predetermined, it won't offer much help. But if you're willing to see things in a new light, I'm here to help you change your perspective through these words.

Consider the concept of a "growth mindset" versus a "fixed mindset," as popularized by psychologist Carol Dweck. A fixed mindset leads to a belief that abilities and intelligence are static, causing a fear of failure and an avoidance of challenges. On the other hand, a growth mindset views challenges as opportunities to learn and grow, believing that abilities can be developed through effort and perseverance. By adopting a growth mindset, you can transform setbacks into stepping stones for personal development.

Perspective is also about recognizing that situations are often temporary. What feels overwhelming today might seem insignificant in a week, month, or year. Understanding this can reduce the intensity of negative emotions and give you a sense of hope and resilience.

To help shift your perspective, try reframing negative thoughts by challenging whether they're based on facts or assumptions. Look for alternative explanations that are more balanced and less emotionally charged. Practicing gratitude regularly can shift your focus to what's right in your life, fostering a more positive outlook. Mindfulness and meditation can help you become more aware of your thoughts and feelings, allowing you to observe them without judgment and choose your responses more deliberately. Seeking perspective from others, whether friends, family, or a therapist, can provide new insights and help you see situations from a different angle. And when faced with a challenge, focus on finding solutions rather than dwelling on the problem—this proactive approach can empower you and reduce feelings of helplessness.

By embracing the idea that you have control over your perspective, you can navigate life's challenges with greater resilience and optimism. This book is here to guide you in shifting your mindset and transforming your life through the power of perspective.

Return on Energy (ROE)

To create the life you've always dreamed of, it's essential to focus on your Return on Energy (ROE). Just like investors seek a return on investment (ROI), we should be mindful of how we spend our energy and what we gain in return. Your energy is a precious resource, and where you choose to invest it directly impacts the quality of your life.

Manifesting your desires hinges on cultivating good feelings, which is why gratitude is so powerful. When you're truly grateful, it's impossible to feel bad. This state of appreciation opens the door to more good things in your life. By focusing on your ROE, you prioritize what brings you the highest positive returns—whether it's joy, productivity, or personal growth.

If you're constantly drained by negative thoughts, toxic relationships, or unfulfilling activities, you're depleting your energy with little to show for it. But when you surround yourself with activities and relationships that uplift you, you recharge your energy, making it easier to chase your dreams and tackle challenges.

Self-care is another vital aspect of ROE. Investing in your physical, mental, and emotional well-being offers high returns. Regular exercise, healthy eating, and practices like meditation or yoga can boost your energy levels and overall happiness, ensuring you have the vitality to pursue what you want.

It's also important to be mindful of what you consume. Whether it's food, media, or information, what you take in directly affects your energy. Choose nourishing foods, limit exposure to negativity, and seek out content that inspires and uplifts you.

Setting boundaries is a powerful way to protect your energy. Learning to say no to people or activities that drain you preserves your energy for what truly matters. It's about recognizing that your energy is finite and choosing to spend it wisely.

Gratitude is the cornerstone of enhancing your ROE. When you focus on what you're grateful for, you shift your perspective from lack to abundance. This positive feedback loop amplifies your energy and aligns you with the flow of good things in your life.

By focusing on your ROE, you create a life that feels balanced, fulfilling, and aligned with your true desires. Manifesting the life of your dreams becomes much easier when you harness the power of positive energy and gratitude, ensuring that you are always in a state to receive more good.

Implementing these strategies allows you to maximize your ROE, leading to a more balanced, fulfilling, and productive life. The key is to be mindful of where your energy goes and ensure it is spent on activities, relationships, and thoughts that bring you the highest positive returns.

Mindset

Have you ever considered that you might be the leader you've been seeking all along? From the time we're young, we're taught to follow the leader—whether it's our parents, teachers, or other authority figures. As adults, we often continue to look to others for guidance, only to find ourselves feeling unsettled or uncertain. But what if the true leader you've been searching for is within you?

I want to share with you the incredible power of mindset and how it can change your life. We all grow up with dreams, but sometimes the doubts and expectations of others can dim our inner light. However, it's crucial to remember that you are the leader you've been looking for all along. You hold the power to choose how you think, act, and feel—and that power is truly transformative.

By embracing this inner leadership, you can guide your life in the direction that feels right for you. You have the strength and wisdom to shape your destiny, make decisions that align with your true self, and overcome any challenge that comes your way. It's time to recognize and trust in your own ability to lead—because you are the leader you've been waiting for.

It's All About Choices

Jim Kwik has a quote that really resonates with me: "Do you know what comes between B & D? C, right? So if B stands for Birth, D stands for Death, and C stands for Choice, it means that as long as you are between

Birth and Death, you get to choose how you think, feel, and respond." This simple yet profound concept underscores that every moment of our lives is shaped by the choices we make.

One of the most powerful choices you can make is to change your thoughts. If you're willing to see things differently, you can shift your mindset to better, more positive thoughts. When negativity creeps in, it's crucial to distract yourself with something uplifting—call a friend, listen to your favorite song, or watch a funny video. These small shifts in focus can have a big impact on maintaining a positive mindset.

Creating new habits, especially when it comes to your thoughts, takes time. Studies suggest it takes about 21 days to form a new habit, so be patient and persistent with yourself. Retraining your brain to think positively doesn't happen overnight, but the effort is well worth it.

When faced with a problem, instead of getting stuck in worry, write it down and brainstorm three possible solutions. This approach shifts your focus from the problem to the solution, empowering you to take control of the situation.

Manifesting is another powerful tool for changing your life and circumstances. Imagine if the only thing you gained from this practice was feeling good 95% of the time—wouldn't that be worth it? True happiness comes from positive, organized thoughts, and manifesting helps you align your thoughts with the life you want to create.

Network Overhaul

Your network plays a pivotal role in shaping your mindset and, ultimately, your life. If you've been struggling to create the life you dream of, it might be time to take a closer look at the people you're surrounding yourself with. I've learned that who you spend your time with can either lift you up or hold you back. If your current circle isn't pushing you to grow or encouraging you to reach for more, it might be time to expand it.

Start by surrounding yourself with people who inspire you—those who are living the kind of life you aspire to have. These are the people who can offer you insights, support, and the encouragement you need. Don't be afraid to reach out to them, even if it feels intimidating at first. Whether it's through networking events, social media, or mutual connections, building relationships with positive, forward-thinking individuals will elevate your own thinking and help you see new possibilities.

It's also important to protect your energy by distancing yourself from relationships that drain you or keep you stuck in old patterns. This doesn't mean you have to cut people out of your life entirely, but be mindful of how much time and energy you're investing in them. Your energy is precious, especially when you're focused on creating a better life, and you need to be intentional about where it goes.

Once you've surrounded yourself with the right people, the next step is to take action. I know it can be scary—trust me, I've been there. The fear of not being qualified enough or worrying about what others might think can be overwhelming. But here's what I've learned: No one starts out feeling completely ready or confident. The key is to take that first step anyway.

Start small. Break down your goals into manageable steps that feel achievable. Each step you take will build your confidence and create momentum. Action creates clarity, and the more you do, the more you'll learn about what works for you and what doesn't. With each step, you'll grow more certain in your abilities.

Growth can be uncomfortable, and that's okay. Whenever you're pursuing something new or challenging, fear and doubt will inevitably creep in. But instead of letting those feelings hold you back, see them as signs that you're on the right path. Growth doesn't happen in your comfort zone, so when you feel uneasy, remind yourself that it means you're pushing your boundaries in the best possible way.

Finally, remember to be kind to yourself and believe in your own potential. Surround yourself with affirmations, success stories, and positive influences that reinforce your belief in yourself. Celebrate your progress, no matter how small, and keep your eyes on the bigger picture. With the right mindset and a strong, supportive network, there's truly no limit to what you can achieve.

This journey is about steady progress, staying true to yourself, and believing in your own power. You've got everything you need within you to create the life you want—it's just about taking that first step and trusting that you're on the right path.

The Placebo Effect

Are you willing to see things differently? If so, let's explore these concepts together and work on transforming your life.

The placebo effect is a powerful reminder that the ability to heal and grow starts in your mind. Think about it—patients often experience real, measurable improvements in their health simply because they believe in the treatment they're receiving, even when that treatment is nothing more than a sugar pill. This belief alone is enough to trigger physiological changes in the body, leading to healing and recovery. It's not the pill that's making the difference; it's the mind's belief in the pill.

Now, imagine applying that same principle to your life. Just as a patient's belief in a placebo can lead to genuine healing, your belief in your ability to manifest your desires can lead to real, tangible changes in your reality. When you hold a strong belief that you can achieve your goals and dreams, your mind starts to work in alignment with that belief. You begin to see opportunities where others see obstacles, and you attract the people, resources, and situations that will help you along your journey.

The truth is that the power to shape your reality lies within you. Your thoughts and beliefs are incredibly powerful—they are the foundation upon which your life is built. When you truly believe in your potential and trust in your ability to manifest the life you want, you set into motion a series of events that bring your desires closer to you.

It's not just about thinking positively or daydreaming about a better future; it's about deeply believing in your own power to create that future. This belief shapes your actions, your decisions, and ultimately, the world around you. It's the driving force behind everything you do, and it has the potential to transform your life in ways you may not have thought possible.

So, if there's one thing to take away, let it be this: Your mind is a powerful tool, capable of shaping your reality. The placebo effect isn't just a medical phenomenon; it's a testament to the incredible power of belief.

Manifesting operates on the same principle. By focusing on positive thoughts, visualizations, and intentions, you can shape your external reality. Regularly visualizing your goals as if they have already been achieved creates a sense of reality, convincing your subconscious mind that these goals are attainable. This mental rehearsal enhances your motivation, increases your confidence, and makes your goals feel more within reach.

Repeating positive affirmations is another powerful practice. Affirmations work similarly to the placebo effect by fostering a mindset that expects success and well-being. When you affirm positive statements about yourself and your capabilities, you gradually shift your self-perception, creating a mental environment conducive to success.

Practicing gratitude is also key. Gratitude shifts your focus from what you lack to what you have, fostering a positive mental state. By regularly acknowledging and appreciating the good things in your life, you train your mind to look for positives, which not only enhances your mood but also aligns you with a higher frequency of positive energy.

Mindfulness and meditation help you stay present and clear-minded, reducing stress and enhancing your ability to focus on your goals. A calm, centered mind is more effective at manifesting positive outcomes, just as a patient's belief in a treatment enhances its efficacy.

Emotions play a crucial role in manifesting. When you align your emotions with your desires—feeling joy, excitement, and gratitude as if your goals are already realized—you create a powerful attractor state. Emotions are a potent form of energy that can amplify your intentions, much like how a patient's positive expectations lead to real health benefits.

The placebo effect shows us that belief and expectation are powerful tools for achieving our goals. By applying these principles to manifesting, you can harness the power of your mind to create the life you want. Just as healing starts in the mind, so does the ability to manifest your dreams. By consciously directing your thoughts, emotions, and beliefs towards your goals, you can transform your reality and achieve the life you envision.

Always remember that the power to shape your life is within you. Every thought, belief, and action you take has the potential to transform your reality. By understanding and harnessing the principles of the placebo effect and manifesting, you can unlock your full potential and craft a life filled with purpose, joy, and fulfillment. The placebo effect shows us just how powerful our minds can be in influencing our outcomes. When we truly believe in something—whether it's a treatment, a goal, or a dream—our minds can turn that belief into reality.

But it's not just about what you believe externally; it's also about how you speak to yourself internally. You are the person you will communicate with the most throughout your life. The conversations you have with yourself, the thoughts you entertain, and the beliefs you hold about who you are and what you can achieve are crucial. That's why it's essential to be kind to yourself. Treat yourself with the same compassion, encouragement, and understanding as you would offer to a close friend.

Becoming your own biggest cheerleader means celebrating your successes, no matter how small, and encouraging yourself through challenges. It means speaking words of positivity and support when you're facing doubt or fear. When you become your own best friend, you create a strong, supportive foundation that helps you navigate life's ups and downs with grace and resilience.

So, as you move forward, take this to heart: the way you treat yourself matters. Cultivate a mindset of kindness, self-belief, and unwavering support for your dreams. With this approach, you'll not only unlock your potential but also build a life that reflects the love and positivity you give yourself every day.

Conclusion

As we come to the close of this section, I want to speak directly to your heart. The power to shape your life isn't something distant or out of reach—it's right there within you. Every thought you nurture, every moment of gratitude you practice, and every ounce of energy you invest with intention is creating the life that reflects your deepest desires. It's not just about what happens to you, but how you choose to think, feel, and respond in every situation. These choices, small as they may seem, are the building blocks of your reality.

Now that you've gathered some practical tools to guide you, the next section is going to introduce you to an entirely new way of seeing things. But before you turn that page, I want you to pause for a moment and ask yourself, "Am I truly ready to see things differently?" If there's even a flicker of willingness within you, then it's time to take that next step with an open heart and mind.

But don't rush past this moment. I want you to truly grasp the incredible power you hold. Your mind is your most powerful ally—use it to craft the perspective that fills you with joy and purpose. Channel your energy in ways that keep you aligned with your true self. And above all, be kind to yourself. Speak words of love and encouragement to the person who needs it most—YOU. After all, you are the one you'll spend your entire life with, the one whose inner voice will echo the loudest.

As you continue on this journey, remember that the only real limit is YOU. You have the ability to break through any barrier, to see beyond any obstacle, and to create a life that's not just lived, but truly cherished. So go ahead, turn the page with confidence, and embrace the transformation that awaits you. Your journey is just beginning, and it's going to be extraordinary.

If you're interested in learning more about me and the work I do to help others, I invite you to visit my website at CFViews.com. I'd love the opportunity to connect and hear your story of transformation.

Renee Vardouniotis

Founder of Mighty Minds Academy

http://www.linkedin.com/in/Renee-Vardouniotis
http://www.facebook.com/renee.vardouniotis
http://www.instagram.com/renee__vee
http://www.mightyminds.us
https://www.5thdegree.com/

With a background as a dedicated Speech-Language Pathologist in public schools, Renee has transitioned into a dynamic Mindset Mentor and Coach, encouraging lasting change in the way we approach challenges and opportunities. As the Founder of Mighty Minds Academy, her commitment is to foster a learning environment that inspires curiosity, critical thinking, and creativity...teaching life lessons for success and fulfillment beyond the lessons taught in the classroom. Through personalized education, innovative teaching methods, and a focus on character development, she aims to nurture well-rounded individuals who are prepared to make a positive impact on society, adapt to challenges, and thrive and excel in an ever-changing world. Renee's transformative journey and strong desire to support families has led her to become a public speaker who leaves a lasting impression and ignite a sense of hope and possibility in all who are in pursuit of a more enriched, successful, and fulfilled life.

The Manifestation Equation

By Renee Vardouniotis

Stealing Thunder

*"I can't tell you what it really is,
I can only tell you what it feels like."*
—Eminem

In an age where self-help books fill entire sections of bookstores and social media is flooded with success stories, the concept of manifesting has captured the imagination of millions. Promising to unlock the secrets of the universe, manifesting suggests that by simply thinking positively and visualizing our desires, we can bring them into reality. I mean, come on, really?! It sounds ridiculous...but is it?

I assume that you are reading this right now because you are wondering if all this manifestation stuff is real. Well, I think it serves us to believe that it is. And what we believe, we become. Isn't it empowering to know that we can intentionally design our lives? What if I said I manifested co-authoring this book? That's a story for later...

The concept of manifestation suggests that our thoughts have a direct impact on the reality we experience. It is based on the belief that by focusing on positive or specific thoughts and intentions, we can bring about desired outcomes in our lives.

Central to the idea of manifestation is the Law of Attraction, which states that like attracts like. If you consistently think positive thoughts and visualize your goals, you attract positive outcomes and opportunities. Conversely, negative thoughts can attract unfavorable circumstances.

To kick this off, I would like to adopt a technique that Eminem used in the movie, *8 Mile*. In the climactic final rap battle scene of *8 Mile*, B-Rabbit (Eminem) faces off against his rival, Papa Doc, in a tense and high-stakes showdown. This scene takes place in a crowded and energetic underground club where the audience's favor can make or break a rapper's performance. Before B-Rabbit takes the stage, he is acutely aware that Papa Doc knows many personal details about his life that could be used against him. Papa Doc wins the coin toss and elects to "let that b_tch go first."

As the beat starts, B-Rabbit seizes the initiative by employing the "stealing thunder" technique, which involves revealing negative facts/information about yourself or a situation before it is mentioned by the opponent or other individuals. B-Rabbit preemptively reveals his own vulnerabilities and challenges, such as living in a trailer park, having personal struggles, and his girlfriend betraying him.

As B-Rabbit raps about his personal life, he simultaneously dismantles any potential attacks Papa Doc might have planned. He shifts the focus onto Papa Doc, mocking him for pretending to be something he is not and questioning his authenticity as a rapper. This not only disarms Papa Doc but also wins over the crowd, who appreciate B-Rabbit's honesty and bravado. By the end of his rap, the audience is firmly on B-Rabbit's side. When it's Papa Doc's turn to respond, he is left speechless, unable to counter B-Rabbit's proactive lyrics. The crowd's reaction solidifies B-Rabbit's victory, as they cheer and celebrate his performance. It is one of the best scenes I have ever seen in a movie.

There is a compelling irony to this story because in real life Marshall Mathers, AKA "Eminem", manifested his way into stardom. Coming from a humble background, with no real direction and no connections to help him become a celebrated rapper, he could have continued to live that simple, unfulfilled lifestyle. Eminem knew he was made for more, and it was his belief in his talents that attracted mentors to work with him to become the famous rapper he is today. Eminem is a perfect example of aligning behavior to make his goal a reality. His ability to overcome struggles, such as addiction and legal issues, and channel them into his music makes him one of the most celebrated rappers in history. Imagine if he didn't believe in manifestation.

I am aware that you may be a skeptic of manifestation and think it's "woo-woo". I hear you. You may have heard information about manifestation that annoys you and you don't believe any of it. The word "manifest" itself may irritate you. You aren't the only one.

Let me "steal the thunder" here. Let's put all the skepticism and criticism regarding manifestation on the table. You can call me B-Rabbit.

Manifestation is often criticized for lacking verifiable evidence to support its claims. Many scientific skeptics argue that there is no concrete scientific basis for the idea that thoughts alone can influence external reality. Some critics view manifestation as a form of magical thinking or wishful thinking. They argue that simply visualizing or affirming desires without taking practical action is unlikely to lead to tangible results.

The concept of manifestation can sometimes be misunderstood or misapplied, leading to unrealistic expectations or disappointment. For example, some people may believe that they can manifest anything they want instantly, without considering the role of effort, timing, and external factors. You can write yourself the "Check from the Universe" but it will not manifest without action towards a goal. Having false hope that magic will happen can lead people to feel ashamed and guilty for not achieving their dreams.

Critics of manifestation believe that factors such as privilege, socioeconomic status, and systemic inequalities play a significant role in determining success and fulfillment. They may attribute apparent manifestations to coincidence, selective thinking, or confirmation bias. They argue that people tend to focus on and remember instances that support their beliefs while ignoring contradictory evidence.

The commercialization of manifestation through books, courses, and seminars has led to skepticism about its authenticity and motives. Some critics view it as a marketing gimmick or a way for individuals to profit from vulnerable individuals seeking solutions to their problems.

Now it's time to disarm the skeptic:

The Law of Vibration is a universal law, just like gravity. Secondary to the Law of Vibration is the Law of Attraction. This idea was popularized by books like the self-help book called *The Secret* by Rhonda Byrne (2006), which claims that thought alone can influence circumstances within one's life. The law is based on the idea that "like attracts like", where we attract what we emit through energy. The book highlights the power of positive thinking; focusing on what you want rather than what you don't and boasts that the three keys to manifestation are "Ask, Believe, Receive". Belief is a powerful force. People are inclined to believe in manifesting, even in the absence of concrete evidence.

While the Law of Attraction emphasizes the power of thought and intentions, it also acknowledges the importance of taking action towards your goals. Manifestation is seen as a combination of thought, belief, and inspired action. Advocates of the Law of Attraction also stress the importance of taking responsibility for one's thoughts, beliefs, and actions. They believe that individuals have the power to shape their own realities through their mindset and behavior.

Some proponents of the Law of Attraction claim that it is supported by principles of quantum physics, suggesting that thoughts and intentions can influence energy and matter at a quantum level. Quantum physics is the study of matter and energy at the most fundamental level. Albert Einstein summarized manifestation powerfully: "Everything is energy and that is all there is to it. Match the frequency of the reality you want, and you cannot help but get into that reality. It can be no other way. This is not philosophy, this is physics."

OK! Now that we have got all that out of the way, let's dive into the compilation of ideas and experiences that I have had and learned about along the way in my life. I continue to discover the relationships between certain foundational concepts and how they relate to manifestation in our lives.

From goal setting and strategic planning to building resilience and nurturing a growth mindset, I am sharing practical and experiential approaches that will empower you to create meaningful change without relying on the uncertain promise of manifestation. I will also tell personal stories of manifestation in my life.

Surrendering to the Flow

"When you become comfortable with uncertainty, infinite possibilities open up in your life." —Eckhart Tolle

As a seasoned Speech-Language Pathologist, I thought I would retire in the field like everyone else, after 30 years of service. I thought this was the path for me, and the dangling carrot of the pension and retirement package seemed to be what everyone looked forward to in the school districts. It was safe and socially praised by most of society. The beginning of my experience in the field began when I decided to stay in New York after graduate school and got my first job at an elementary school in Elmont, Long Island. This was in 2002, and the school district was opening its first Applied Behavior Analysis (ABA) classes for students with Autism. I gladly accepted the job as the sole speech therapist for this population and understood that we were building a brand-new program. I was excited by the challenge and eager to learn. I was also looking forward to my future with the love of my life, Ianni, the reason why I stayed in New York and didn't move back home to Pennsylvania.

After 4 years of working with children on the spectrum with very high-level needs, I began to develop migraines. My body was speaking to me, and I followed my intuition to take care of myself and make a change. I decided it was time to spread my wings and work with the "typical" population of students. I met with the Director of Special Education and requested a move. I had faith that this was the right thing to do for me, even though I felt bad about leaving my students and the staff members in that program.

At first, I was intimidated by planning therapy for the new students on my caseload. I felt like I was starting a completely new job. I was transferred to another elementary school in the district (for some, this kind of move is a nightmare). For me, I was ready for a change. It turned out to be an easy transition to the school, which was dubbed "the country club" out of the six schools. I began to feel a new flame of motivation and determination to master my craft. For the next eight years, I worked in several of the elementary schools in that district; each time, finding my way around a new building, new students, new staff, new principal, new expectations, new office, and a new schedule. I didn't fear these moves, I had a belief that I would grow as a human and therapist by the new experiences (good and bad) that were presented.

In 2013, tragedy struck my family in a way that changed my whole life. I was pregnant with my daughter and driving home from a bachelorette party when I got the call. My sister's husband, someone I considered a brother, did not wake up that morning. This sent my whole world upside down. I would go into the sad details, but I want to focus on the reason why I am telling you this. This led to a paradigm shift for me. After I had my daughter, I began thinking that I wanted to move near my sister and parents. Life just seemed better in Pennsylvania. Easier. My flame for working in that district in New York was dimming, and I knew intuitively that I needed to make another move.

In 2015, I got a call from my sister. She was eager and excited to tell me that there was an opening for a speech therapist in her school district in Pennsylvania. At first, I laughed it off. I mean, I had a job, a home, my friends, my husband's job, and my kids to consider. I wasn't even licensed in Pennsylvania.

I couldn't sleep that night. The Universe was sending me a sign. What are the chances that the perfect job would magically appear for me? I began to think about how incredible it would be to move near my family. To have my children raised around their cousins and grandparents. So, I started the overwhelming process of getting my Speech-Language Pathology license in Pennsylvania, transferring all my documents over, and applying for this position at the new school. The interview process was grueling, but I knew deep down this was the career and life move that would be most aligned with whom I was growing into at the time.

The mere thought of moving and uprooting my family was nerve-racking, confusing, and overwhelming. I knew, though, I just knew if I got through the short-term hard process, it would be so worth it in the long term. I pushed through the terror barrier of making the decision to take the job. Ironically, the same night I signed the contract committing to the new district, my sister got engaged to a new man. The juxtaposition was palpable. Here, my grieving sister was experiencing joy and excitement, and I was in a room contemplating my future, by myself, and a ball of nerves. It turned out to be the best decision I ever made.

Ironically, it can be said that my sister manifested her new relationship. She had a vision of what she wanted her life to look like after the death of her husband. This was a quick process. She decided that she would have an open mind about meeting someone new and allowing him to be her partner and co-parent her children. There were certain non-negotiables that she set, and her new relationship met every single one. It didn't take time, it took alignment. Her story is a testament to believing in the unseen and having faith... Manifestation at its finest!

The amount of change I experienced in my adult life would make many uncomfortable. People tend to stay where things are familiar and "safe." If nothing changes, nothing changes. Consistently putting ourselves in uncomfortable positions allows us to adapt to the feeling of unease. It becomes more manageable, and the results of the discomfort are the rewards of an exciting and fulfilled life.

Patience and Trusting the Process

> *"Manifestation is not about forcing the universe to bend to your will but trusting that what you desire is on its way."* —Unknown

In three weeks, I found myself saying goodbye to my friends and neighbors, packing my kids up, and moving to Pennsylvania. We rented a townhouse, set up childcare for my daughter, registered my son for 1st grade, and I started my job right after. My family's support and guidance were integral during this time. My husband, Ianni, stayed in New York to work and came down on the weekends. It was funny; although he was initially resistant to the move, I found our marriage became stronger throughout this transition. When Ianni visited on the weekends, we were able to have a great time together because we were renting and didn't have all the responsibility of home ownership. We began to expand our social circle to friends that we only were able to visit when we lived in New York. Weekends were fun, exciting, and jam-packed with events, family, and friends. A whole new world opened up.

Ten months later, after selling our house in New York and finding a new job, Ianni moved to Pennsylvania. We began to house hunt. The market was hot at that time, and it seemed that a house went on the market and was immediately sold. None of those homes were ours, and I knew it. My intuition spoke to me, and I had a vision of the type of house I wanted. There was always something "wrong" with each house we toured. I remember some people saying that we "would never find the perfect house," to which my response was always, "Yes. I will."

The day I saw my house and went inside, I just knew. It was the perfect layout, location on the street, finished basement, and endless possibilities to decorate and make ours. I called Ianni to come see it. The couple selling the house endured a contentious divorce, so they were extremely motivated to sell. They accepted our offer, and we were on our way to home ownership in Pennsylvania. I still pull up to my neighborhood and house and say, "I love it here."

Embracing Challenges as Opportunities

"In the midst of chaos, there is also opportunity."
—Sun Tzu

A year after moving into our home our daughter, Mila, who was three at the time, began exhibiting some odd behaviors. At times, she would look up and stare and then do a little shimmy shake. At first, we joked about it, and I would tell people that she was chatting with our favorite people who had crossed over. Considering the open wound that was my brother-in-law's death was still raw, I felt comfort in thinking he was speaking to her. That strange behavior began progressing into longer stares, stronger shaking, and vocalizations that sounded like "mumm mumm mumm." Peter, ever the sweet older brother, would say, "I think Mila is hungry!" My instinct was telling me differently, I just didn't know what it could be. As the weeks went by, the occurrence of these behaviors became more frequent, and we took Mila to the emergency room. She was then admitted, where we spent the next five days. Our baby was wired up and plugged into a wall in the hospital room, where the neurologists could read her brain waves. It was determined that Mila was having seizures and was diagnosed with Epilepsy. It was like we were hit by a Mac truck. A medicine regimen began, and her behavior became belligerent. At one point, she threw Play-Doh right at my mom's head and laughed hysterically when it hit her! Who was this child?? The seizures were still frequent, and we documented each episode for weeks after we got home from the hospital. We finally found the right medicine cocktail for her, and the seizures waned. She was doing better, but I wasn't. I was experiencing major anxiety and felt like I couldn't function at home or work. I didn't feel clear. It was like my head was a balloon on a string floating above me. I knew I had to be okay for my family and my job, so I consulted a doctor and went on anxiety medication. It saved me.

During the months after the diagnosis, I began feeling an immense gratitude that Mila's seizures were under control, and she was able to live a normal life as a preschooler. It was during this time that I discovered a love for philanthropy and give-back. This manifested a connection with a lady who sold ONEHOPE Wine. I hosted a wine tasting at my home to support the Epilepsy Foundation, honoring my little warrior and all the other children challenged with neuroatypicality. I quickly fell in love with the mission and vision of ONEHOPE (plus I love wine) and joined the team. From there, I hosted hundreds of wine tastings and online fundraisers to support various causes. I am still a part of ONEHOPE today, and proud of it.

Tending to the Soul's Garden

"The only limits that exist are the ones you place upon yourself."
—Bob Proctor

I grew up always wanting to do big things. Unfortunately, I wasn't confident enough to follow through on my own vision of how I wanted to show up in the world. I cared too much about what others thought. One of the main lessons I have learned throughout my years is that we can't care what others think. We need to please ourselves and follow our hearts. I remember fantasizing about being on TV, singing on stage, dating a famous actor, or becoming best friends with someone famous that could launch me into a bigger world. The desire for this ebbed and flowed for many years, even into my adulthood. I had these amazing ideas of inventions that I thought would solve problems and make me millions. I envisioned becoming "known." This is not an easy thing to do in a world of eight billion people.

When I dove into personal development and learned that we can do, have, or be anything we want, my quest for this notoriety skyrocketed. I listed all the things I wanted and made my vision board. During this time, I invested thousands into things like e-commerce, Shopify stores, direct sales companies, wine companies, and other potential interests. I thought I was going to make it big in one of these areas. Boy was I wrong. I ended up racking up my credit cards just seeking a way to become "someone." I then met a friend in my mastermind program that I connected with like we were friends for our whole lives. We shared a common interest in bringing personal development to the youth, as we were both educators seeking to make an impact further and wider (and outside of the invisible jail that we called "work"). We wanted to become a chain link to the family tree of pioneers in the personal development industry. But we had a different approach. We wanted to create mindset and empowerment programs for the youth, something that was not done yet. We started a company and began developing programs. We got our LLC, website, and logo done. We were ecstatic about the potential of this company and how we would make so many lives better (and make so much money doing it). We then trademarked and got our programs copywritten and developed a cartoon script. I thought to myself...this is IT. I am going to be SOMEONE. We developed an actual product that was amazing, however, we overspent and weren't able to sell it. We had a team of folks interested in helping us on this mission and movement towards a brighter future for the youth. Eventually, our inconsistent leadership and flying by the seat of our pants was not making anyone money, and we were losing money by the day.

One investment we decided to make was in speaker training. I am so grateful we did. I knew that speaking on stage was the most powerful way to spread a mission and vision. We eventually had a presentation professionally done by a major speaker in the industry. I felt prepared and official. My excitement began to increase at this point because the reaction to the incredible vision was well received. I figured now I could book events and speak on stage to get the word out there. My business partner, however, was not as excited to put herself out there. I was READY. I began seeking opportunities to speak at events and booked my first presentation in New York City. When I arrived there, I was nervous, but I knew my presentation inside and out. It was a good thing I did, because the technology wasn't working so I had to make my speech on the fly, without the visuals. Still, I loved the spotlight. It was so exciting for me to be in front of the crowd, expressing my big goals and mission. The premise of what we created was well received, as the response from the attendees was overwhelmingly positive. That was the proverbial funeral eulogy for my partnership with my business partner.

Understanding that I was making a shift out of my first company, I knew I had to keep the momentum going. In a matter of a month, I got to reinvent myself and my brand. When thinking about what to name my new company, I wanted it to be meaningful, powerful, and catchy. While researching names, I was reminded of the nickname my son, Peter, was given as an elementary school football player. His coaches nicknamed him "Mighty." I didn't think much about it then. I knew they called most of the players by their last names and Peter's last name was a mouthful so they gave him a name they could easily shout out! It meant so much more than that, I know that now. The word "mighty" means having great strength, power, or influence. It can describe someone or something that is exceptionally powerful, strong, or impressive in size, scope, or intensity. My son, Peter, embodied this describing word in so many ways. Not only did the nickname stick for his four-year football career, but it also empowered him to become that caliber of athlete. He now plays high school basketball and continues to believe in himself and his capabilities. It's amazing how words affect our children. We should think about that more as we are raising them. Words have power, and they can stick to us like glue whether they are positive or negative. Often someone's opinion of us becomes our reality when we don't have a strong self-image and sense of worth.

Mighty Minds Academy was born out of a passion and conviction that I can help families shift generational programs that may not be serving them. Most of us are programmed to be negative. Having a Mighty Mind suggests that we can all be exceptionally insightful, understand complex ideas, solve difficult problems, and think critically. Mighty Minds Academy emphasizes the strength and competence of one's mental faculties. This type of education is about raising awareness and gaining clarity on our potential as humans. It's about practicing persistence, consistency, and breaking fear barriers...all of which I am actively utilizing while writing this chapter!! Children often mirror our characteristics, behaviors, and emotions because they frequently observe us and absorb our way of life. They can reflect both our positive and negative traits, as well as our habits and reactions to various situations. When we begin noticing negative behavior in our children, it is a signal that we need to work on ourselves and our emotions. We can use this as an opportunity for self-improvement and growth to become better parents and role models for our children. It's a simple concept, yet so undervalued. We would rather pay academic institutions for knowledge and continuing education that feeds us more information, but not invest in our personal development. Why??

I figured out it was because I was in the wrong environment. I needed to surround myself with like-minded people who spent more time developing themselves than on continuing education. Those who are "awake" to understand the importance of mindset and how it affects every facet of our lives. Everyone needs this type of education! Well, I found my circle in the form of a huge event in Nashville.

I booked a spot to speak at the Impact Effect Conference. I had the opportunity of a lifetime to present my story and my dream of bringing personal development to families and teens. It was a miracle that I ended up in that lineup of speakers! This time, I was on an actual big stage with lighting, photographers, videographers, and a room full of hundreds of people. I shared a stage with Tim Storey, Coach Burt, Brian Galke, Craig Siegel, and other giants in the speaker circuit. Imposter Syndrome was not even the word to describe how I felt. It was one of the most incredible experiences of my entire life. When I look back at that time, I realize that I finally was doing what I dreamt about my whole life. To do big things. I am now friends with those incredible speakers, and we are collaborating on events and making a big impact, together.

Visualizing Your Goals

"See the things that you want as already yours. Know that they will come to you at need. Then let them come. Don't fret and worry about them. Don't think about your lack of them. Think of them as yours, as belonging to you, as already in your possession."
—Robert Collier

Manifestation comes in different ways. We can have a vision of what we want, but we may end up receiving something similar or better than what we envisioned. Most people don't recognize or appreciate this. I can think of a few times that this happened to me as I was growing up. When I turned 16, I could not WAIT to drive. I got my license as soon as I could, took the car, and took off! I was seeking this freedom for a long time in my early teen years. My father, bless his heart, gave me his old car. The blue Pontiac 6000LE. I didn't care what I was driving then if I could leave my house and go where I wanted. Great memories were made driving that car, but as time went on, I desired to drive something more updated and "cool." This especially became more of a desire as I was graduating high school. My friends had cute, small, and newer cars and I began to feel a little embarrassed by my grocery-getter.

I applied to Penn State University, and I was awarded a full scholarship to attend there. At first, I didn't understand how incredible this was. When we are 17, the concept of how much money our parents spend is not at the forefront of our minds. My father offered me half of what he would have spent for me to go to Penn State. This was exciting! Guess what I did? You got it, I bought a new car! It wasn't the expensive one I always dreamed of, but it was new and cute and small, like my friends had. In the years after I graduated college, I invested in driving amazing and luxurious cars. I will always appreciate having that first set of wheels, but I will not make my kids drive cars that make them feel embarrassed.

You could also say that I manifested my way into living in New York City. While applying to graduate programs, I had an interest in several schools in New York. I also applied to some in Pennsylvania (more so to please my parents). At the time, the Graduate Record Exam (GRE) was required to apply to graduate schools. Historically, I had not been a stellar standardized test taker, and this one was no exception. I took it twice and could not meet the mark that graduate schools require. I did not get into any of the grad schools that I applied to, except New York University. That left me with really no choice about where I would be living! After interviewing at the clinic, I received my letter of acceptance. I moved to Manhattan, the concrete jungle where dreams were made, and I felt excited and hopeful. Connecting the dots backwards, the Universe had my back. One important concept I have learned in my life is that nothing that is meant for you will pass you by. It makes sense how this all worked out for me.

I have also unintentionally manifested. After I moved back to Pennsylvania we bought our house, and I was using my old vacuum. I love to vacuum and do it often. The vacuum I had was a plug-in and it began to annoy me. It was a little heavy and the cord would not reach very far. I kept thinking that once this vacuum goes, I am going to treat myself to a cordless vacuum. One that I can use on wood floors and carpets. For a few weeks, I thought about this and was going to begin researching which one I would get. One day, I went outside to check the mail and there was a box on my driveway. Since we get deliveries from Amazon every other day, I didn't think twice about it. I opened the box. Wouldn't you know it, inside was a cordless vacuum. I thought my husband ordered it for me as a surprise and I got excited. I called him to thank him, and he

didn't know what I was talking about! Then I glanced at the mailing label, and I didn't recognize the name on it and it wasn't addressed to my house. Oh, man!! What are the chances of this? I called Amazon and was told it was their mistake and that I could keep that vacuum. They were going to send another vacuum to the original address. I couldn't believe it... It was like this gift from above landed on my driveway. I still use that vacuum every day.

It's funny, I mentioned it before... I manifested co-authoring this book. Throughout my personal development experience, I have done extensive research, hired several coaches, been on several podcasts, and spoken to several people. The relationships I am building with like-minded folks are invaluable and the conversations we have are rich with possibilities, ideas, and collaborations. The programs I have developed are rooted in purpose, backed by science, and based on research that has studied the top 1% of performers in the world. The people I have attracted as friends, partners, and coaches are all privy to this information. In fact, I am speaking at an event called the 1% Event this year. This is no coincidence!

I knew one day I would like to write a book; however, I didn't think I could find the time and resources to do it with everything I had going on with my Academy and my family. Then, one day, the opportunity presented itself through a key relationship that I now have, and here we are! This is the perfect beginning of my author experience, sharing it with the incredible co-authors in this book.

Now I would like to focus on how certain areas of our lives are related to manifestation. This may resonate with you in ways you never thought about! My hope is to raise your awareness. When we shift our beliefs and focus, magical things happen!

THINKING INTO A MIGHTY MIND

The Relationship Between Mindset and Manifestation

The concept of manifesting is intricately tied to mindset. Supporters of manifesting often emphasize that a positive, proactive mindset is crucial for attracting desired outcomes. There is a deep connection between mindset and manifesting. Our beliefs, attitudes, and mental states influence the manifestation process.

At the core of manifesting is the principle of positive thinking. This idea, popularized by figures like Norman Vincent Peale in *The Power of Positive Thinking*, suggests that maintaining an optimistic outlook can significantly impact one's reality. Positive thinking is believed to elevate mood, enhance motivation, and increase resilience, all of which are seen as essential for manifesting goals.

Manifesting often involves techniques like visualization and affirmations, which require individuals to mentally picture their desired outcomes and repeat positive statements. Cognitive reframing, a psychological technique where individuals change the way they perceive situations, plays a critical role here. By visualizing success and repeating affirmations, people may reframe

their mindset to focus on possibilities rather than limitations. This shift can lead to increased confidence and a greater willingness to pursue opportunities.

Carol Dweck's concept of the growth mindset is highly relevant to the discussion of manifesting. According to Dweck, individuals with a growth mindset believe their abilities and intelligence can be developed through effort and perseverance. This belief aligns with manifesting's emphasis on the power of belief and intention. A growth mindset encourages individuals to see challenges as opportunities for growth, thereby fostering the kind of proactive, resilient attitude that manifesting advocates consider crucial.

Self-efficacy, or the belief in one's ability to succeed in specific situations, is another key component linking mindset to manifestation. High self-efficacy can enhance motivation and persistence, crucial for turning visions into reality. Manifesting practices often aim to boost self-efficacy by encouraging individuals to focus on their capabilities and potential for success.

The placebo effect, where belief in the effectiveness of a treatment can lead to real physiological improvements, illustrates the power of belief on outcomes. Similarly, self-fulfilling prophecies, where an individual's expectations about a situation can cause those expectations to come true, highlight how mindset can shape reality. These phenomena suggest that believing in the effectiveness of manifesting can indeed influence one's behavior and, consequently, their outcomes.

While a positive mindset can be empowering, an overemphasis on positivity can sometimes lead to detrimental effects. Toxic positivity, where individuals feel pressured to maintain a positive outlook despite genuine challenges, can prevent them from processing negative emotions and addressing real issues. Additionally, an exclusive focus on positive thinking can lead to neglecting practical actions and realistic planning, which are essential for achieving goals.

For manifesting to be truly effective, a positive mindset must be complemented by actionable steps. Setting realistic goals, creating strategic plans, and maintaining disciplined effort are necessary components of success. Manifesting should be viewed not as a replacement for hard work, but as a tool that enhances motivation and direction.

The Relationship Between Self-Love and Manifesting

Self-love and manifestation are deeply intertwined concepts that reinforce and amplify each other. Manifesting, at its core, requires a foundation of self-belief and self-worth, both of which are cultivated through self-love.

Self-love involves recognizing one's intrinsic worth, embracing self-compassion, and nurturing oneself both physically and emotionally. It is about valuing oneself regardless of external

achievements or validation. When individuals practice self-love, they build a strong sense of self-worth and confidence, which are crucial for effective manifesting.

Manifesting relies heavily on the belief that one deserves to achieve one's desires. If an individual lacks self-love and consequently self-worth, they may subconsciously sabotage their manifesting efforts. Feelings of unworthiness can create mental blocks that hinder the manifestation process. Therefore, cultivating self-love helps remove these barriers, allowing individuals to fully embrace and act upon their desires.

One of the common techniques in manifesting is the use of positive affirmations. These are statements that individuals repeat to themselves to reinforce positive beliefs and intentions. Affirmations like "I am worthy of success" or "I deserve love and happiness" can significantly boost self-love by ingraining these positive beliefs in the subconscious mind. This enhanced self-love, in turn, supports more effective manifesting by aligning one's mindset with their goals.

Visualization, another key technique in manifesting, involves mentally picturing oneself achieving desired outcomes. When combined with self-love, visualization becomes even more powerful. Visualizing oneself succeeding not only reinforces belief in one's capabilities but also nurtures self-compassion by focusing on one's potential and strengths rather than limitations. This practice encourages a kinder and more supportive inner dialogue, which is essential for both self-love and manifesting.

Limiting beliefs, often rooted in a lack of self-love, are thoughts that constrain what individuals believe they can achieve. Examples include beliefs like "I am not good enough" or "I don't deserve success." Self-love helps to challenge and dismantle these limiting beliefs by nurturing a deeper acceptance and appreciation of oneself. As these negative beliefs are replaced with more empowering ones, individuals find it easier to manifest their desires.

The relationship between self-love and manifesting is reciprocal. While self-love enhances manifesting, the process of manifesting can also promote self-love. Achieving small goals through manifesting can boost self-esteem and reinforce the belief that one is capable and deserving. Each success, no matter how small, builds confidence and self-love, creating a

positive feedback loop that makes further manifesting even more effective. Here are practical strategies to cultivate self-love:

Practice Self-Compassion:

- Treat yourself with the same kindness you would offer to a friend in times of need.
- Replace self-criticism with self-compassion when you make mistakes or face setbacks.

Set Healthy Boundaries:

- Learn to say no when necessary to protect your time and energy.
- Respect your personal space and emotional limits.

Self-Care Activities:

- Dedicate time to self-care activities that nurture your body, mind, and soul.
- This can include meditation, exercise, hobbies, or simply relaxing with a good book.

Positive Affirmations:

- Use positive affirmations to challenge negative self-talk.
- Remind yourself of your strengths and capabilities.
- Repeat affirmations like "I am enough," "I love and accept myself unconditionally," and "I deserve happiness."

Surround Yourself with Positivity:

- Choose to be around people who uplift and support you.
- Limit exposure to negative influences or toxic relationships.

Practice Gratitude:

- Regularly reflect on the things you're grateful for in your life.
- Appreciating the good can boost your self-esteem and self-love.

The Relationship of Our Thoughts and Manifesting

The concept of manifestation suggests that our thoughts have a direct impact on the reality we experience. It is based on the belief that by focusing on positive or specific thoughts and intentions, we can bring about desired outcomes in our lives. Here's a deeper look into how our thoughts relate to manifestation.

Central to the idea of manifestation is the Law of Attraction, which posits that like attracts like. If you consistently think positive thoughts and visualize your goals, you attract positive outcomes and opportunities. Conversely, negative thoughts can attract unfavorable circumstances.

Our thoughts direct our attention and focus. By thinking about what we want to achieve, we prime our minds to notice opportunities and resources that align with our goals. This mental focus can enhance our ability to take actions that move us closer to our desired outcomes. Thoughts shape our beliefs, and our beliefs influence our actions. If we believe that we can achieve something, we are more likely to take the necessary steps to make it happen. Manifestation encourages cultivating a positive belief system that supports our goals.

Thoughts generate emotions, and emotions can fuel our motivation and persistence. When we think about our goals with positive emotions, such as excitement and joy, we are more driven to pursue them, even in the face of challenges.

Visualization is a key technique in manifestation. By vividly imagining the achievement of our goals, we create a mental blueprint that guides our subconscious mind. This practice can increase our confidence and reduce anxiety about the future.

Our thoughts can create self-fulfilling prophecies. If we expect success, we are more likely to engage in behaviors that lead to successful outcomes. Conversely, expecting failure can lead to behaviors that fail. Manifestation is not just about thinking positively but also about aligning our actions with our thoughts. Taking consistent, purposeful action towards our goals is essential for manifestation to work effectively.

Manifestation encourages a growth mindset, where challenges are seen as opportunities for learning and growth. This mindset shift can lead to greater resilience and perseverance.

The relationship between our thoughts and manifestation lies in the power of our mental focus, belief systems, emotions, and actions. By consciously directing our thoughts towards positive outcomes and taking aligned actions, we can influence our reality in meaningful ways.

The Relationship Between Goal Setting and Manifesting

Goal setting and manifestation are closely related concepts that work synergistically to help individuals achieve their desired outcomes. Understanding their relationship and significance can empower people to turn their dreams into reality. The power of goal setting and manifestation lies in their ability to transform desires into tangible outcomes through a structured yet holistic approach. Goal setting involves defining clear, specific, and measurable objectives, and providing a concrete plan and direction. This clarity is essential for creating a roadmap to success. Manifestation complements this by focusing on visualizing and believing in desired outcomes, utilizing the power of positive thinking and the law of attraction to bring these goals into reality. Effective goal setting emphasizes creating actionable steps and strategies to achieve objectives, requiring discipline and commitment to follow through with the plan. Manifestation enhances this process by aligning thoughts, emotions, and actions with the desired outcomes, encouraging inspired action that feels in harmony with the vision.

Goal setting and manifestation are complementary practices that, when integrated, can significantly enhance the ability to achieve desired outcomes. Goal setting provides the structure and direction, while manifestation empowers the mindset and emotional alignment necessary for success. Together, they create a powerful framework for turning dreams into reality.

Integrating Goal Setting and Manifestation

- Begin with clear, specific goals that outline what you want to achieve. Use goal-setting techniques to create a structured plan. Regularly visualize your goals as already achieved.
- Cultivate a deep belief in your ability to manifest these goals. Combine structured, actionable steps with inspired actions that feel right and resonate with your vision.

- Keep a positive and expectant attitude, focusing on gratitude and the belief that your goals are within reach.
- Regularly review your progress, celebrate achievements, and make necessary adjustments to your plan and mindset.

The Relationship Between Confidence and Manifesting

Confidence fuels the belief that your goals and desires are achievable. When you have confidence in yourself and your abilities, you are more likely to believe that you can manifest what you want. This belief is a key component of the Law of Attraction, which predicates that believing in your goals attracts them into your reality. Confidence plays a crucial role in the process of manifesting desired outcomes. It acts as a bridge between your goals and their realization.

Confidence contributes to a positive mindset, which is essential for manifesting. A positive mindset aligns your thoughts and emotions with your desires, helping to attract positive outcomes. Confident individuals focus on opportunities and solutions rather than obstacles, enhancing their ability to manifest their goals.

Exercising confidence drives action and persistence, which are critical for manifesting. Believing in yourself encourages you to take the necessary steps towards your goals and to persevere despite setbacks. This proactive approach increases the likelihood of turning your desires into reality.

Confidence emits a higher vibrational energy, which is crucial in the process of manifesting. The Law of Attraction suggests that like attracts like, so maintaining a high vibrational frequency through confidence and positivity helps to attract similar high-vibration experiences and outcomes.

Confidence helps to overcome fear and doubt, which can be major barriers to manifesting. Fear and doubt can create negative energy that blocks the manifestation process. Confidence mitigates these negative emotions, allowing you to focus on your goals with clarity and determination.

Confident individuals engage in effective visualization and affirmation practices. Confidence enhances the vividness and emotional intensity of visualizations, making them more powerful. Similarly, confident affirmations reinforce positive beliefs about achieving your goals.

Confidence can attract opportunities and resources that aid in manifesting. People are drawn to confident individuals, which can lead to valuable connections, collaborations, and support. This network of opportunities can significantly accelerate the manifestation process.

Confidence is closely tied to a sense of self-worth and deservingness. Believing that you deserve good things increases your ability to manifest them. This sense of deservingness aligns your internal beliefs with your external desires, creating a harmonious pathway for manifestation.

Confidence is a powerful catalyst in the process of manifesting. It enhances belief in possibility, fosters a positive mindset, drives action and persistence, raises vibrational frequency, helps overcome fear and doubt, improves visualization and affirmation practices, attracts opportunities,

and reinforces self-worth. By cultivating confidence, you strengthen your ability to manifest your goals and create the life you desire.

Practical Tips to Build Confidence for Manifestation

- Start with small goals that are easy to accomplish. Each success will build your confidence and create momentum for bigger manifestations.
- Use positive affirmations to reinforce your self-belief and confidence. Statements like "I am capable of achieving my

dreams" can boost your confidence and align your thoughts with your desires.

- Regularly visualize yourself achieving your goals. This practice not only enhances your belief in your ability to succeed but also aligns your subconscious mind with your desired outcomes.
- Confidence grows through action. Take steps toward your goals, no matter how small. Each action taken reinforces your confidence and brings you closer to manifesting your desires.
- Engage with people, environments, and activities that uplift and support you. Positive influences can boost your confidence and keep you motivated on your manifestation journey.

The Relationship Between Bravery and Manifesting

The relationship between bravery and manifestation is powerful, as both concepts involve overcoming internal and external challenges to achieve desired outcomes. Taking risks helps break through fear and limiting patterns that can hold you back from achieving your dreams. It opens up new possibilities that you might not have considered, breaking the cycle of repetitive, unproductive behaviors.

Bravery involves facing and overcoming fears and doubts, requiring us to step out of our comfort zone and confront uncertainties. It involves the courage to continue despite setbacks, failures, or obstacles. The path to manifestation is rarely smooth, and bravery provides the strength to persist, helping maintain a commitment to a vision even when faced with challenges. During the process of manifestation, fears and doubts often arise, and bravery helps overcome these mental blocks. Taking bold actions empowers individuals to take decisive actions toward their goals, even when the outcome is uncertain. Manifestation requires taking actionable steps, and bravery ensures these steps are taken, regardless of how daunting they may seem. It often requires exploring new and uncertain territories and embracing change instead of fighting it.

Bravery and healthy risk-taking empower individuals to take initiative, turning ideas and dreams into concrete actions. Without bravery, hesitation, or procrastination may delay the manifestation process. Each brave action creates momentum, building confidence and reinforcing commitment to goals.

Manifestation requires not just thoughts and beliefs, but also actions. Taking risks shows a serious commitment to your goals. It signals to yourself and the universe that you are dedicated to achieving your desires, no matter what. This level of commitment often leads to a higher investment of energy and resources into your goals, enhancing the likelihood of manifestation. Healthy risk-taking can raise your vibrational energy by aligning your actions with your highest intentions, attracting similar positive energies and outcomes. When you take risks that align with your goals, you become a magnet for opportunities and resources that help you achieve those goals.

Practical Ways to Cultivate Bravery for Manifestation

- **Challenge Yourself**: Aim for goals that push your boundaries. Stretch goals encourage you to step out of your comfort zone and build bravery.
- **Forgive Mistakes**: Be kind to yourself when you face setbacks or failures. Self-compassion helps you maintain courage and continue moving forward.
- **Positive Outcomes**: Regularly visualize yourself successfully achieving your goals. Visualization reinforces bravery by making the desired outcome feel more attainable.
- **Incremental Risks**: Begin with small acts of bravery and gradually take on bigger challenges. This approach builds confidence and reduces the fear of failure.
- **Positive Influence**: Engage with people who encourage and

support your goals. A positive support network can boost your bravery and resilience.

- **Recall Bravery**: Reflect on times when you were brave and succeeded. Reminding yourself of past successes can inspire and reinforce your current efforts.

The power of thought, belief, and intentions cannot be denied. These are powerful tools to align our inner world with our outer desires. By understanding, developing, and applying these ideas, we can bring magic into our reality. The practice of manifesting is not just about achieving outcomes but living our lives with a greater sense of fulfillment, joy, and connection to the world around us.

It is my hope that, if you are a naysayer, I have given you a reason to revisit your belief in these ideas, and possibly open your mind a bit. You may be satisfied and content with the way your life is unfolding, but I promise you that intentional manifesting will only make your life better.

My other hope is that, if you are a believer, you have been inspired to continue to practice the tools provided that will allow your dreams to become reality. You deserve the best and don't ever listen to anyone tell you something different.

Rhonda Byrne, of the Secret, said it best: "Eliminate all doubt and replace it with the full expectation that you will receive what you are asking for." We should follow her lead, as well as all the others who are living lives we dream of having. They are proof that manifestation is not bullshit. The gap between the life you want and the life you are living is called mindset, focus, and consistency.

Lastly, I want to state that contrary to popular opinion, we don't only live once. We only die once. We live every day. Make it count!

Sonny Von Cleveland

Founder and CEO of The Von Cleveland Foundation

https://www.linkedin.com/in/sonny-von-cleveland-541415299/
https://www.facebook.com/sonnyvoncleveland8x
https://www.instagram.com/sonnyvonclevelandofficial/
https://www.tvcfoundation.org/
https://www.heywhiteboy.com/

Mr. Sonny Von Cleveland is a motivational speaker and author, renowned for his profound ability to inspire and heal through sharing his own transformative journey. As the founder of The Von Cleveland Foundation, he dedicates himself to providing coaching, resources, and a nurturing learning environment. His work extends to mentoring disenfranchised youth in Southern California's juvenile facilities and collaborating with Boo2Bullying and the Anti-Recidivism Coalition in Los Angeles, focusing on youth development.

Raised in Michigan, Mr. Von Cleveland's early life was fraught with challenges, including severe trauma and a subsequent period of incarceration. His experiences, detailed in his moving memoir, "Hey White Boy - Conversations Of Redemption," serve as a testament to the power of redemption and personal growth. His commitment to positive change and his ability to turn adversity into a source of empowerment make him a beacon of hope and a true agent of change in today's society.

From Chains To Change

By Sonny Von Cleveland

The question: Is Manifesting Bullshit?

Here's my answer:

My name is Sonny Von Cleveland, I'm a motivational speaker and author. My life's mission is to share my history and experiences with abuse and incarceration to help others heal and find their path to growth and transformation. My story is not just one of overcoming adversity but also of discovering the power of manifesting the life I have now. From being a victim of molestation and violence during my childhood to spending eighteen years in incarceration, my journey has been filled with significant challenges. However, through the power of manifestation and personal development, I transformed my life and now dedicate myself to aiding and inspiring others.

In this section, I aim to explore the concept of manifesting through the lens of my life experiences. Many people debate whether manifesting is real or just wishful thinking. By sharing my story, I hope to provide a deeper understanding of how manifesting can play a pivotal role in personal transformation. My journey from a troubled youth to a motivational speaker and coach is a testament to the power of manifesting one's dreams and aspirations. I invite you to join me as we delve into my life story and uncover the truths about manifesting.

I was born into a family that struggled with many issues. From an early age, I faced significant hardships that shaped my worldview. My childhood, from age five until I was ten, was marred by molestation and violence at the hands of multiple men. These traumatic experiences left deep scars and a sense of confusion about my place in the world. I didn't know how to process the pain and fear that consumed me. The feeling of being trapped in a cycle of abuse and neglect became my reality.

As a child, the constant fear and anxiety felt like a prison, and I was left with no tools to cope with the overwhelming emotions. The abuse not only destroyed my ability to trust others but also planted deep-rooted feelings of worthlessness within me. I began to internalize the belief that the world was a cruel and unsafe place, and as a result, I withdrew from it. I built emotional walls so high that nobody could penetrate them. My relationships with others were shallow because, at my core, I believed that no one could be trusted. This distrust wasn't just of strangers or acquaintances—it extended to family, friends, and even myself.

One of the earliest coping mechanisms I developed was dissociation—mentally checking out when things got too intense. This detachment provided a temporary escape from the horrors of my reality. I would go numb, convincing myself that nothing mattered because, in my mind, I didn't matter. As a result, my self-esteem became nonexistent. I believed I had no inherent value beyond being an object for others to exploit.

I vividly remember the fear and helplessness I felt as a child. The constant state of anxiety and the inability to trust those around me created a barrier between me and the world. I developed coping mechanisms to survive, but these mechanisms often led me into further trouble, like being convicted of my first felony at age seven. The trauma I experienced had a profound impact on my development. I found myself repeatedly in trouble with law enforcement, unable to escape the cycle of violence and crime that my early experiences had ingrained in me. By the age of sixteen, I was incarcerated, beginning an eighteen-year sentence that would see me entrenched in a violent gang lifestyle as a means of survival.

My teenage years were a blur of survival tactics and trying to find some semblance of control in a world that seemed bent on my destruction. The streets and the prison system became my battlegrounds, and gang life became my shield. I was lost, angry, and convinced that this was my destiny.

However, even in the darkest times, some moments and individuals influenced my journey. One such pivotal moment came in my late twenties when I was sent to solitary confinement for five years. It was there that I met a Muslim man who changed the course of my life. Through his guidance, I began to learn the power of forgiveness and letting go of the past. This man introduced me to the concept of manifesting a new reality for myself, planting the seeds of a transformation that would take years to fully realize.

Growing up in an environment filled with abuse and violence, I never believed in God or the concept of manifesting. My life experiences made it hard to accept that there could be any higher power or that I had any control over my destiny. The idea of manifesting seemed like a cruel joke to someone who had seen only the worst of humanity. I was living a life that was a direct reflection of my mindset—a mindset shaped by fear, anger, and survival.

It wasn't until much later, reflecting on my past, that I understood that my mindset had indeed been manifesting my reality. The constant negativity and expectation of violence and betrayal created a self-fulfilling prophecy. I was attracting the very things I feared and despised because my thoughts were consumed by them. This realization was both shocking and enlightening. I began to see the power of thoughts and beliefs in shaping one's life.

My first real exposure to the concept of manifesting came during my time in solitary confinement. The Muslim man who mentored me introduced me to the idea that our thoughts and beliefs could shape our reality. At first, I was highly skeptical. How could thinking positively change a life that had been nothing but hardship and suffering? But with nothing to lose and a desire to find some semblance of peace, I decided to give it a try.

One of the most difficult aspects of my journey was learning how to let go of my past trauma. It's one thing to talk about forgiveness and healing, but it's an entirely different matter to actually confront those demons and make peace with them. My past was filled with so much pain, anger, and betrayal that, for years, I thought the only way to survive was to hold onto that rage. It became my armor, protecting me from the world, but it was also the very thing that was destroying me from the inside out.

Forgiving the people who hurt me seemed impossible at first. How could I forgive men who stole my innocence, who shattered my trust in humanity, and left me with a lifetime of scars? Every time I tried to think about forgiveness, it felt like I was betraying myself—as if forgiving them meant that what they did was okay. But deep down, I knew that holding onto this hatred was like carrying a burning coal, hoping it would hurt the other person. In reality, I was the only one getting burned.

The truth is, I almost gave up on forgiveness many times. There were moments when the pain of my past was so overwhelming that it felt easier to continue being angry and bitter. I would convince myself that I didn't need to forgive anyone, that I could keep moving forward without ever letting go of the anger. But the more I tried to ignore it, the more it consumed me. There was a constant battle between wanting to let go and not knowing how and between wanting to heal and feeling like I didn't deserve healing.

I remember being in solitary confinement and having days when I would just sit in that tiny cell, the walls closing in on me, thinking about the people who had hurt me. The memories would come flooding back, and with them, all the emotions I had been trying to suppress for so many years. I would sit there, fists clenched, shaking with anger at the injustice of it all. I wanted to scream at the top of my lungs, to hit something, anything, just to get the rage out of my body. But there was nothing I could do. There was no release. It was just me and the memories.

That's when I realized that I was still a prisoner—long before the bars went up around me. I was imprisoned by my own hatred, by my refusal to forgive. I was trapped in the past, living every day with the weight of those experiences hanging around my neck like a chain. If I wanted to be free, truly free, I had to find a way to break that chain.

But forgiving others was just one part of the battle. The even harder part was learning to forgive myself. I carried so much guilt and shame over the choices I had made, over the life I had lived. I blamed myself for not being stronger as a child, for not fighting back harder against my abusers. I blamed myself for the hurt I caused others in my rage-filled years. I blamed myself for becoming the very thing I despised: a person who hurt others because of my own pain.

That self-blame was a heavy burden to bear. Every time I thought about my actions, about the harm I had caused, the people I had wronged, I felt like I was unworthy of forgiveness. How could I forgive myself when I had done so much damage? There were days when I believed that I didn't deserve a second chance, that the person I had become was beyond redemption. The guilt weighed on me like a thousand pounds, crushing any sense of hope I had for a better future.

There were moments in that isolation, staring at the concrete walls, where I thought about giving up entirely. The mental and emotional exhaustion of carrying my past was suffocating. The pain was so overwhelming at times that it felt like a wave crashing over me, pulling me under, making it hard to breathe. I was tired—tired of fighting, tired of surviving, tired of the endless cycle of anger and guilt. There were days when I wanted to close my eyes and not wake up, to escape from it all once and for all. But something inside me wouldn't let me go. As much as I struggled, there was a small voice in the back of my mind, whispering that I was worth more, that I could find a way out if I just kept pushing.

That's when I started to see forgiveness not as something I was doing for them, but for me. Forgiveness wasn't about excusing their actions or pretending it didn't hurt—it was about reclaiming my power. It was about freeing myself from the prison I had built around my heart. Holding onto that pain was keeping me shackled to the past, and I couldn't move forward until I let it go.

Forgiveness didn't happen overnight. It was a slow, painful process. Every time I thought I had forgiven someone, a memory would resurface, and all the anger would come rushing back. I had to learn that forgiveness is not a one-time event; it's a choice you have to make over and over again. Each time the pain came back, I had to consciously choose to let it go again. It was exhausting, but it was necessary.

I also had to learn to forgive myself in the same way. I had to accept that the mistakes I made, and the harm I caused, didn't define me. They were part of my journey, but they didn't have to be my identity. I started to understand that I was doing the best I could with the tools I had at the time. The choices I made were rooted in the trauma I had endured, and while I wasn't responsible for them, I could also choose to grow from them. Self-forgiveness was about giving myself permission to be human, to be flawed, and to move forward without being held hostage by my past.

Letting go of the trauma that had shaped me for so long was like removing a heavy cloak I had worn for years. At first, I felt exposed without it, vulnerable. The anger and resentment had been my armor, and without them, I wasn't sure who I was. But slowly, I began to realize that by letting go, I wasn't losing anything—I was gaining the freedom to define myself on my own terms, not through the lens of my trauma.

Forgiveness, both for others and for myself, became the cornerstone of my transformation. It allowed me to break free from the mental prison that had held me captive for so long. It opened the door to healing, growth, and the possibility of a future I had never thought possible. In letting go of the past, I was finally able to move forward and start manifesting the life I truly wanted.

One of the first steps in my journey was learning to forgive and let go of the past. This was incredibly difficult, as my life had been defined by anger and resentment. Through hours of introspection and guided meditation, I slowly began to release the hold that my past had on me. This process was painful but necessary. I started to notice small changes in my attitude and interactions with others, even within the harsh environment of prison.

Encouraged by these small victories, I began to consciously attempt to manifest more significant changes in my life. I focused on visualizing a future where I was no longer a victim of my circumstances but a person in control of my destiny. My first attempts were met with mixed results. Some things improved, while others remained stubbornly unchanged. However, I started to see a pattern—the more I believed in the possibility of change, the more likely it was to occur.

Looking back, those early attempts at manifesting were crucial learning experiences. They taught me that manifesting is not about wishing for things and expecting them to happen overnight. It's about changing your mindset and aligning your actions with your goals. It's a continuous process of self-improvement and belief in one's potential. The more I practiced, the more I realized that my previous life of abuse and violence was a manifestation of my inner turmoil. Changing my inner world was the key to changing my outer reality.

Receiving five years in solitary confinement was a test of endurance and mental fortitude. Each day in isolation pushed me to the brink, forcing me to confront my deepest fears and unresolved trauma. Initially, the oppressive solitude seemed like an unending punishment, a stark reminder of the bleak reality of my situation. The isolation compounded my feelings of hopelessness, making it difficult to envision any form of escape from this dark chapter of my life.

During these trying times, the concept of manifesting seemed more like a cruel illusion than a feasible strategy for change. My past experiences had conditioned me to anticipate the worst, casting a shadow over any glimmer of hope. Yet, the teachings from my mentor in solitary confinement began to resonate with me. I gradually realized that my internal conflict was a barrier to embracing the transformative potential of manifesting.

After 19 months in solitary confinement, a moment of clarity washed over me, marking the beginning of a profound shift in my life. Every day spent in isolation had pushed me closer to my breaking point, forcing me to confront the shadows of my past—the fear, the pain, and the unresolved trauma that had haunted me for so long. The walls around me were thick, but the emotional walls I had built were even thicker. It was during one particularly dark moment, lying on the cold floor of my cell, that the lessons from my mentor began to resonate more deeply. He had once said, "Your mind can be your prison, or it can be your path to freedom. It's up to you." The words didn't click until I was stripped of every external distraction, left only with my own thoughts.

Teaching the class became a pivotal moment in my life. It provided a tangible example of how manifesting could transcend current circumstances. As I prepared and conducted my lessons, I saw firsthand the impact of positive visualization and focused intention. The inmates responded enthusiastically, and I felt a renewed sense of purpose. This experience reinforced my belief in the power of manifesting and demonstrated that by aligning my thoughts with my desires, I could create significant changes in my reality.

This opportunity to teach was not just a break from solitary confinement but a validation of my ability to manifest a better future. I began to focus on visualizing my life beyond prison, imagining a path filled with purpose and fulfillment. The success of my teaching efforts further solidified my belief in the principles of manifesting. By concentrating on what I wanted—growth, connection, and positive impact—rather than what I lacked, I started to attract opportunities that aligned with my goals.

The transformation in my mindset was profound. The opportunity to teach highlighted the power of manifesting to influence not only my external circumstances but also my internal state. By shifting my focus from scarcity to abundance, I opened myself up to new possibilities. This realization became the cornerstone of my journey and is a message I now share with others: The power to change our lives lies within our thoughts and beliefs.

When I was released in 2016, I set my sights on becoming a musician. Despite having no prior training or experience, I refused to let limiting beliefs hold me back. Music had always been a passion of mine, and I felt that it could be a powerful outlet for my emotions and experiences. Within nine days, I created a band, and within 90 days, we were signed to a label. This rapid success was a powerful testament to the effectiveness of manifesting when you have no limiting beliefs.

My journey into the music world was a whirlwind. I remember the excitement of our first practice sessions, where raw energy and creativity flowed freely. We poured our hearts into our music, writing lyrics that spoke to our experiences and hopes. The process of recording our first album was both challenging and exhilarating. It was during this time that I fully embraced the idea that our thoughts and beliefs truly shape our reality. I visualized success, not just for myself but for the entire band, and I witnessed how our collective belief in our potential brought us opportunities we could only dream of.

Touring was another significant milestone. Each performance was a manifestation of our hard work and dedication. We played in various cities, connecting with audiences who resonated with our message. The experience of being on stage, feeling the energy of the crowd, and knowing that our music touched people's lives was incredibly fulfilling. It reinforced my belief that when you focus on what you want and remove any doubts, you can achieve extraordinary things.

The onset of the COVID-19 pandemic in 2020 brought many challenges, but it also presented new opportunities. With live performances halted and the world in lockdown, I had to find new ways to stay creative and connected. I decided to become a YouTube creator. The idea of building a channel from scratch was daunting, but I was determined to make it work.

I started by creating content that was authentic and engaging, sharing my journey and insights on various topics. I visualized my channel growing and reaching a wide audience. Within 90 days, my channel grew to 50,000 subscribers. This was yet another proof of the power of manifestation. By focusing on my goals and putting in the necessary work, I was able to achieve significant growth in a short period. The key was to maintain a positive mindset and adapt to the changing circumstances.

My success on YouTube opened new doors. I was able to connect with a global audience, share my story, and inspire others. The feedback and support I received from viewers were overwhelming. It reinforced the idea that when you believe in yourself and your vision, you can overcome any obstacle. The pandemic, which initially seemed like a setback, turned out to be a catalyst for new opportunities and growth.

Deciding to move to California marked another significant chapter in my journey. I focused on working towards my life's purpose and began manifesting my dreams into reality. California represented a new beginning, a place where I could fully pursue my passions and make a difference. I wrote my book, built a cat café, and started a photography business. I also established my nonprofit organization, which is dedicated to helping others overcome adversity.

The recognition I received, including Congressional, Senate, and other awards, as well as being named Palm Springs Person of the Year 2023, served as further evidence of the power of manifesting. Each accolade was a testament to the hard work, dedication, and positive mindset I maintained throughout my journey. These achievements were not just personal victories but also validation that manifesting works.

Through these experiences, I learned several important lessons about manifesting:

- **Clarity and Focus:** Being clear about what you want and maintaining focus on your goals is crucial. When your vision is clear, it's easier to align your actions and thoughts towards achieving it.
- **Action and Belief:** Manifesting requires not only a strong belief in your goals but also consistent action towards achieving them. Belief without action is futile. You need to take concrete steps towards your dreams.
- **Overcoming Limiting Beliefs:** Letting go of limiting beliefs opens up new possibilities and allows for greater achievements.

It's essential to recognize and challenge any negative thoughts that hold you back.

- **Adapting to Change:** Embracing change and seeing opportunities in challenges can lead to unexpected successes. Flexibility and resilience are key components of manifesting.

These lessons have shaped my approach to life and continue to guide me as I pursue my goals. Manifesting has proven to be a powerful tool in my personal growth and has enabled me to achieve things I once thought were impossible. The journey of self-discovery and growth is ongoing, and I am excited to see what the future holds as I continue to manifest my dreams into reality.

When I decided to start my businesses, including a cat café and a photography business, I was met with a wave of skepticism and criticism. People around me often shared horror stories about the difficulties of entrepreneurship. They spoke of high failure rates, financial struggles, and the relentless challenges that come with starting and running a business. Friends, family, and even well-meaning acquaintances questioned my decisions, often advising caution and suggesting that I might be setting myself up for disappointment.

Despite the naysayers, I held steadfast to my beliefs and my vision. I had seen the power of manifesting work in my life before and was confident it would work again. I knew that if I allowed myself to be swayed by doubt and negativity, I would be undermining my goals. Instead of letting the criticism deter me, I used it as motivation to prove to myself and others that my dreams were achievable.

Starting the cat café was a particularly ambitious endeavor. I envisioned a space that would not only serve as a haven for cat lovers but also promote animal adoption and provide a unique community experience. The logistical challenges were immense—from finding the right location and navigating health regulations to securing funding and creating a business plan. Critics were quick to point out the potential pitfalls, suggesting that the idea was too niche or financially risky.

However, I believed in the concept and its potential impact. I focused on manifesting success, visualizing a bustling café filled with happy customers and cats finding loving homes. I broke down the seemingly insurmountable task into manageable steps, tackling each challenge with a positive mindset and unwavering determination. The power of my belief and the clarity of my vision helped me navigate the complexities and bring the cat café to life.

While maintaining a strong belief in manifesting, I also understood the importance of practical action. Manifesting is not about wishful thinking; it's about aligning your thoughts and actions with your goals. I meticulously planned each aspect of my businesses, conducting thorough research and seeking advice from experienced entrepreneurs. By combining belief with practical strategies, I was able to build a solid foundation for my ventures.

For the photography business, I knew that talent and passion alone wouldn't be enough. I invested in high-quality equipment, honed my skills through continuous learning, and networked with other professionals in the industry. I visualized successful photo shoots and happy clients, but I also put in the work to ensure I delivered exceptional results. This blend of manifesting and practicality allowed me to establish a reputable and thriving photography business.

Every entrepreneurial journey comes with its share of setbacks, and mine was no different. There were times when things didn't go as planned— financial challenges, marketing missteps, and unexpected obstacles. Instead of viewing these setbacks as failures, I saw them as opportunities for growth and learning. I reminded myself that manifesting was not a magic wand but a powerful tool that required resilience and adaptability.

Each setback taught me valuable lessons. I learned to pivot and adapt my strategies, to seek creative solutions, and to remain focused on my long-term vision. By maintaining a positive mindset and refusing to be discouraged by temporary setbacks, I turned challenges into stepping stones towards success.

To maintain a balance between belief in manifesting and practical reality, I developed daily practices that reinforced my mindset. I started each day with meditation and visualization exercises, focusing on my goals and envisioning positive outcomes. Affirmations played a crucial role in keeping my beliefs strong, and my mind focused on success.

Additionally, I surrounded myself with a supportive network of like-minded individuals who believed in the power of manifesting. Engaging with mentors, attending workshops, and participating in mastermind groups provided both inspiration and practical insights. This community helped me stay grounded, motivated, and accountable.

Finally, I embraced the principle of continuous improvement. Manifesting is an ongoing process that requires constant refinement of thoughts, beliefs, and actions. I regularly evaluated my progress, set new goals, and adjusted my strategies as needed. By committing to lifelong learning and growth, I ensured that my approach to manifesting remained dynamic and effective.

Throughout my journey, one fundamental truth has emerged: the power of belief. If you think manifestation is real, it is. If you think it is not, then it is not. This simple yet profound philosophy has guided me through the darkest times and the most challenging endeavors. Your mindset shapes your reality. If you believe you can achieve something, you will find a way to make it happen. Conversely, if you think you can't, you will encounter obstacles that confirm your doubts.

I invite you to embrace the possibility of manifesting in your own life.

Believe in your potential and visualize the life you want to create. Remember, your thoughts are powerful tools that can shape your reality. Whether you are striving to overcome adversity, pursue a passion, or achieve a dream, manifestation can be a powerful ally on your journey.

Here are some tips and strategies to help you harness the power of manifestation:

1. **Set Clear Goals:** Be specific about what you want to achieve. Clear goals provide direction and focus, making it easier to align your thoughts and actions with your desired outcomes.
2. **Visualize Success:** Spend time each day visualizing your goals as already achieved. Picture yourself living the life you desire, feeling the emotions of success and fulfillment.
3. **Use Positive Affirmations:** Reinforce your beliefs with positive affirmations. Statements like "I am capable of achieving my goals" or "I attract opportunities for success" can help shift your mindset.
4. **Take Action:** Manifestation is not just about thinking positively; it requires action. Take concrete steps towards your goals, no matter how small. Each step brings you closer to your vision.
5. **Overcome Limiting Beliefs:** Identify and challenge any negative beliefs that hold you back. Replace them with empowering thoughts that support your goals.
6. **Stay Resilient:** Setbacks are part of any journey. Use them as opportunities to learn and grow. Maintain a positive mindset and stay committed to your vision.
7. **Practice Gratitude:** Cultivate an attitude of gratitude for what you have and what you are working towards. Gratitude can attract more positive experiences into your life.
8. **Surround Yourself with Positivity:** Build a support network

of like-minded individuals who believe in your potential. Engage with mentors, join communities, and seek inspiration from others who have achieved similar goals.

To deepen your practice of manifestation, consider incorporating these techniques and exercises into your daily routine:

1. **Journaling:** Keep a manifestation journal where you write down your goals, visualizations, and affirmations. Document your progress and reflect on your journey. This practice can help reinforce your intentions and track your growth.

2. **Vision Boards:** Create a vision board filled with images, quotes, and symbols that represent your goals and dreams. Place it somewhere visible to serve as a constant reminder of what you are working towards. The visual representation can strengthen your commitment and focus.

3. **Meditation and Mindfulness:** Practice meditation and mindfulness to quiet your mind and connect with your inner self. These practices can help you stay present, reduce stress, and enhance your ability to visualize and manifest your goals.

4. **Gratitude Rituals:** Develop daily gratitude rituals, such as writing down three things you are grateful for each morning or evening. This practice can shift your focus from what you lack to what you have, fostering a positive and abundant mindset.

5. **Affirmation Cards:** Create a set of affirmation cards with positive statements that resonate with your goals. Draw a card each day and focus on the affirmation, repeating it throughout the day to reinforce your belief in your abilities.

6. **Goal-Setting Workshops:** Participate in goal-setting workshops or create your own goal-setting sessions. Break down your long-term goals into smaller, manageable steps and create action plans. Regularly review and adjust your goals as needed.

7. **Accountability Partners:** Find an accountability partner who

shares similar goals and values. Check in with each other regularly, share progress, and offer support and encouragement. Having someone to hold you accountable can boost your motivation and commitment.

Common Misconceptions About Manifestation

It's Just Wishful Thinking:

- Manifestation is often misunderstood as mere wishful thinking. However, it is a proactive process that combines positive thinking with deliberate action. It's about creating a mindset that supports your goals and taking steps towards achieving them.

It's Instant Magic:

- Many people expect immediate results from manifestation, but it's not a magic wand. Manifestation requires time, effort, and patience. It's a journey of growth and alignment, where persistence plays a vital role.

It's Only for Material Gains:

- While many use manifestation to achieve material success, it can be applied to any area of life—health, relationships, personal growth, and more. The principles of manifestation can help create a balanced and fulfilling life in all aspects.

Manifesting has profoundly shaped my life, transforming my dreams into reality and guiding me through adversity. By believing in the power of your thoughts and taking purposeful action, you, too, can harness the power of manifestation. Trust in your potential, embrace the journey, and watch as your life transforms in remarkable ways. Remember, the power to create the life you desire lies within you.

Manifestation is the practice of thinking aspirational thoughts with the purpose of making them real. In essence, it is the process of bringing something tangible into your life through attraction and belief. If you believe it, visualize it, and work towards it, you can manifest it. This concept is grounded in the law of attraction, which posits that like attracts like. Therefore, positive thoughts attract positive outcomes, while negative thoughts can bring about negative experiences.

While manifestation might seem like a mystical concept, there is a psychological basis for it. The power of positive thinking and visualization can influence your actions and attitudes, leading to tangible results. Cognitive psychology supports the idea that our thoughts and beliefs shape our behaviors. By focusing on positive outcomes, we are more likely to engage in behaviors that lead to those outcomes. This is often referred to as the self-fulfilling prophecy.

Neurologically, visualization can enhance performance. Athletes and performers use mental imagery to improve their skills and outcomes. By visualizing success, the brain rehearses the act, creating neural patterns that mirror actual performance. This makes the act of achieving the goal feel more familiar and attainable.

Manifestation is a powerful tool for transforming your life. It's about aligning your thoughts, beliefs, and actions with your deepest desires. By setting clear intentions, visualizing success, using positive affirmations, taking inspired action, maintaining a positive mindset, practicing gratitude, and trusting the process, you can manifest your goals and create the life you envision.

So, the question: Is manifesting bullshit? The answer is this: If you think it is, then it is. If you believe it is the key to everything in life, then you, my friend, have your answer.

Norma Cavazos

Harlandale ISD
School Board Trustee, SMD4

https://www.facebook.com/norma.a.perezcavazos
https://normacavazos.scentsy.us/

Norma is a mother of two adult children. She have been married for almost 25 years and serve on various Boards and Committees. She wear many hats.

By day, Norma serves as a Paralegal at the prestigious Rosenblatt Law Firm. She host a podcast called "A Servant's Heart", where she shares inspiring stories and insights.

Her dedication goes beyond her professional life. She hold the position of Trustee SMD4 for the Harlandale ISD School Board, working hard to ensure the best education for students.

Additionally, Norma recently got appointed to the Board Texas State University Parent & Family Advisory Council. She is a member of the Pan American Women League of San Antonio. She also serve on the Advisory Council for a non profit organization, Women Unlimited! SA, She is a Scentsy Consultant, and an elected Precinct Chair.

My New Journey Traveling on the Road of Manifestation

By Norma Cavazos

For those of you who may not quite fully process this concept, let me just tell you that I was one of you not too long ago, until I put it to the test, accepted it, and began to practice everyday life with it.

Manifestation, as defined by Merriam-Webster Dictionary, is the "process of making something visible or concrete." In other words, it's the act of turning thoughts into reality.

The process of bringing our thoughts, desires, or intentions into reality through belief and focused action, allowing us to shape our lives consciously, not just passively accepting what comes our way. This concept of manifestation has gained popularity recently. It is important to understand that emphasis on personal responsibility can be detrimental. When we fail to manifest our desired outcomes, the blame is often internalized, leading to us feeling inadequate and self-doubt. This can easily create a vicious cycle of negative self-talk and hinder personal growth. Rather than empowering individuals, manifestation can foster a culture of blame and shame.

Through manifestation, we can make ourselves happier and healthier, and create positive changes in the world around us. What we cannot fully accept is the fact that the most crucial aspect of manifestation lies in our very own everyday thoughts. Every second, we communicate with our mind, telling it what to do. We send messages to the universe about our desires and intentions. By changing our thoughts, we can change our lives. It is said that the law of attraction operates on this principle: like attracts like.

Our energy influences the outcomes we experience. The hardest part for me was to learn to stay focused and consistent, and trust the process that a positive train of thought will result in positive results. It was important for me to learn to be clear about goals and intentions. Whether a romantic relationship, career success, or health improvement, I needed to learn to define and be specific as to what I truly desired.

I began to search for and read articles about how the universe responds to the energy I emit. How it all aligns with my thoughts, emotions, and actions and I then learned how that power will shape my reality. By mastering my thoughts, I could attract anything I wanted to grasp.

Manifestation began to empower me in a way of consciously creating a fulfilling life aligned with my passions and purpose. By practicing positive thinking, setting clear intentions, visualizing my desires, and taking inspired action, I manifested improved health and happiness. Through intentional manifestation, I attracted meaningful relationships in my personal and professional life. By focusing on what I truly wanted, I transformed my social connections. This newfound way of my thoughts shifted my mindset from scarcity to abundance. I was determined to also attract financial opportunities, career growth, and wealth by aligning my thoughts with pure prosperity. It wasn't just wishful thinking; it was a deliberate process that would profoundly impact every aspect of my life and that of my husband and children.

A few years ago, I was stuck in a job that drained my energy. I decided to apply the principles of manifestation. I visualized myself in a fulfilling role, surrounded by supportive colleagues. I set clear intentions and took inspired action—networking, updating my resume, and attending events with like-minded individuals, all focusing on the same thing— throwing into the world positive energy, so that the world could throw it back at us. Within months, I received an unexpected job offer that aligned perfectly with my desires. It was a career breakthrough that transformed my professional life and proved yet again the definition of manifestation.

I then took it a step further—not always easy to do, but I needed to remain focused on being consistent and trusting the process of the energy I was releasing into the world, I decided to shift gears and begin to set goals for financial abundance: I shifted my mindset from scarcity to abundance. Instead of worrying about bills, I affirmed financial prosperity. I visualized money flowing into my life. Unexpected freelance opportunities and a promotion at work followed. While it wasn't instant, the consistent practice of positive manifestation led to increased financial stability. Am I now rich? Do I have more money than I know what to do with? Of course not! However, somehow, I always have more than I did before and a little more than I assumed I would have, and money seems to easily stretch.

I am getting older every day. I do not know the secret of the fountain of youth, and so with age comes worries about my health. I found myself silently in my mind, obsessed over symptoms that I had been experiencing, and as a human being with flaws, I could not help but start to fear the worst. Unsurprisingly, my anxiety exacerbated physical discomfort. It was a powerful lesson for me to learn as well. I realized that negative thoughts could manifest as real physical sensations. I shifted my focus to wellness and gratitude, and my health improved.

I share with those around me who are willing to have an open heart and open ears, that inside us, we hold the possibilities we create for ourselves, but we also hold the hurdles that can keep us from obtaining our wishes, dreams, and goals. Negative self-talk affects confidence. When you begin to convince yourself that you are not good enough for certain opportunities, you are telling the world that it should turn its back on you.

Just as positive attracts positive, negative attracts negative. As a result, you will miss out on promotions, travel experiences, and creative projects. You must consciously change your inner dialogue. Positive affirmations boost self-esteem, and when this happens, you then begin seizing opportunities that you previously did not ever think were attainable.

Again, what you emit to the world is what the world will shower you with. Negative expectations will influence behavior and create unnecessary conflicts. Through self-awareness and intentional manifestation, we must trust the process of manifestation and communicate openly with only a positive mindset. Manifestation is a powerful tool that shapes our reality. Whether positive or negative, our thoughts have immense creative potential.

Article after article, they were all the same. Each spoke about the art of Manifestation. The art of bringing one's desires into reality through focused intention and belief. One that would allow me to align my deepest passions and purpose. It was not at all easy to begin this new journey of unchartered waters, but I knew that life was passing me by, and that I did not have anything to lose by merely jumping on this path with an open mind and open heart, and just seeing where it would take me. Would it make a believer or non-believer out of me? The only way to find out was to put it into practice.

My journey began with a simple yet profound shift toward positive thinking. I learned to cultivate a mindset that fostered optimism and gratitude, which became the fertile ground for planting the seeds of my future. This change in perspective was not merely about ignoring life's challenges but about facing them with a constructive attitude. It was a conscious choice to focus on solutions rather than problems and to see opportunities instead of obstacles.

With a positive mindset, I set clear intentions for what I wanted to manifest in my life. These intentions were not vague wishes but specific, actionable goals. I articulated my desires for health and happiness with precision, knowing that clarity is the first step toward realization. My intentions served as a compass, guiding my thoughts and actions toward my desired destination.

Visualization was the next step in my manifestation practice. Each day, I dedicated time to vividly imagine my life as I wanted it to be, engaging all my senses to make the experience as real as possible. I saw myself full of vitality, engaging in activities that brought me joy and fulfillment. I felt the happiness that would come from living a life aligned with my values and aspirations. This mental rehearsal acted as a blueprint for my thoughts and aligned my beliefs with my goals.

While positive thinking, intention-setting, and visualization laid the groundwork, it was inspired action that brought my desires into reality. I listened to my intuition and took steps that felt aligned with my goals. Whether it was adopting healthier eating habits, incorporating regular exercise, or seeking out activities that nurtured my well-being, each action was a deliberate choice toward manifesting my ideal state of health and happiness.

The culmination of these practices led to a noticeable improvement in my health and overall well-being. I found myself more energetic, more resilient to stress, and more engaged with life. My relationships flourished, my career took on new meaning, and I discovered a sense of peace and contentment that had previously eluded me. It was as if the universe conspired to assist me, presenting opportunities and resources that aligned with my intentions. This personal story is a testament to the potential of manifestation when approached with sincerity and effort. It can be a powerful tool for personal transformation by aligning my thoughts, emotions, and actions with my desired outcomes.

This concept has often been associated with attracting wealth and prosperity. For many, including myself, the journey of manifestation has been a transformative experience that shifted the mindset from one of scarcity to one of abundance. I soon realized that aligning my financial thoughts with the energy of prosperity can open doors to financial opportunities and career growth. I was constantly worried about finances, feeling trapped in a cycle of lack and limitation. The fear of not having enough led to a constricted view of life, where opportunities seemed scarce and the future uncertain. This mindset was not only debilitating but also self-perpetuating, as it kept me in a state of stress and anxiety, more times than I want to admit, and unable to see beyond my immediate circumstances.

The discovery of manifestation principles was a turning point. I learned about the Law of Attraction and the power of the mind to influence reality. Skeptical at first, I decided to give it a try, as I had little to lose and much to gain. I started with small affirmations, declaring my openness to abundance and my worthiness to receive it.

Gradually, I began to shift my focus from what I lacked to what I could create. I visualized myself succeeding, being in a position where financial worries were a thing of the past. I imagined the feelings of security and freedom that would come with financial abundance. This mental shift was crucial, as it allowed me to align my thoughts with the notion of prosperity.

As my mindset changed, so did my reality. Opportunities that I had previously overlooked began to present themselves. I stumbled upon a side project that turned into a lucrative side gig. It was as if the universe was responding to my new outlook on life, providing me with chances to grow and prosper. The result of this mindset shift was tangible. Not only did my financial situation improve, but I also experienced a sense of empowerment. I no longer felt like a victim of circumstance but rather a creator of my destiny. My career took on a new trajectory, one that was aligned with my aspirations and values.

Manifestation is more than just achieving goals. It's about personal empowerment. By taking control of your thoughts and beliefs, you gain a sense of agency over your life. It fosters self-confidence, resilience, and a positive outlook. This new journey involves practical steps:

- **Self-Love and Acceptance**: Manifestation begins with self-love. Accepting yourself unconditionally is essential for attracting positive experiences.
- **Personal Growth**: Manifestation encourages personal growth and development. As you work toward your goals, you expand your capabilities.
- **Creating a Better World**: By focusing on positive manifestations, you contribute to a collective shift in consciousness, creating a better world for everyone.

Manifestation is not always a linear process. Obstacles and setbacks are common. To overcome these challenges, you must:

- **Persistence**: Keep believing in your goals, even when faced with difficulties.
- **Self-Doubt**: Challenge negative thoughts and replace them with positive affirmations.
- **Patience**: Manifestation takes time. Be patient with the process.
- **Flexibility**: Be open to unexpected opportunities and adjustments to your plans.

The potential impact of adopting an abundance mindset through manifestation is bigger than your thoughts, goals, or desires. It shows that when we change our internal dialogue from scarcity to abundance, we can attract prosperity in various forms. While manifestation is not a magic wand that instantly changes reality, it is a powerful tool for personal transformation, influencing our perception and, consequently, our life's path.

Although it is often thought of as merely wishful thinking, my experience and the experiences of many others suggest that it is far more than that. I found that it is an intentional process that, when approached with discipline and clarity, can profoundly impact every facet of my life.

While grand manifestations like winning the lottery or finding your soulmate often grab headlines, the true power of manifestation lies in its subtle, everyday applications. Positive thinking and intention can manifest into positive experiences. Some of the simplest thoughts of positivity can bring you some of the joyous moments in everyday situations. Manifesting a parking spot can lead to unexpectedly finding a convenient space. Focusing on desired weather conditions can increase the likelihood of experiencing them. A positive attitude can attract pleasant and unexpected encounters.

For years, I viewed life as a series of random events, a chaotic dance of circumstances beyond my control. That was until I encountered the concept of manifestation; not as a mystical secret, but as a practical process grounded in clear intention and focused energy. For me, it began as a structured practice. Each morning, I would sit in quiet reflection, setting my intentions for the day. I articulated my goals, not just in terms of outcomes, but also in the qualities I wished to embody. Patience, resilience, kindness—these became my mantras, my guiding stars.

As I aligned my thoughts with my values, I noticed a shift in my actions. Decisions became easier to make, not because the options were simpler, but because I was clearer on what mattered most to me. Opportunities arose that were not only lucrative but also deeply fulfilling, as they resonated with my innermost desires.

The most profound impact of manifestation was on my personal relationships. By focusing on the energy I brought into interactions, I fostered deeper connections with those around me. I became more present, more attentive, and more authentic. The quality of my relationships improved, reflecting the values I had been manifesting internally.

On a physical level, manifestation guided me toward a healthier lifestyle. I visualized myself as vibrant and whole, which led me to make choices that supported that vision. I adopted a more nutritious diet, engaged in regular exercise, and prioritized rest. My health improved, not by chance, but by the deliberate application of my intentions.

The changes in my life did not go unnoticed. Friends and family began to inquire about the transformation they observed. As I shared my journey of manifestation, I saw the ripple effect of inspiration. Others started to apply these principles, creating their realities that reflected their deepest desires and values.

It is a powerful process that, when engaged with purpose and commitment, can touch every aspect of our lives. By directing our thoughts and energy with intention, we can indeed craft a reality that mirrors our aspirations and honors our values.

Trust the process! Manifestation involves several key steps: setting clear intentions, believing in the possibility of achieving them, visualizing the desired outcome, and taking inspired action. Believe that this process aligns the individual's energy with the universe, thereby attracting opportunities and resources that can help realize your goals.

While having a positive outlook is beneficial, action is necessary to achieve goals. Although the debate over whether manifestation is legitimate or "bullshit" is still ongoing, there are psychological benefits to positive thinking and visualization. The concept of manifestation may oversimplify the path to achieving goals. It is essential to recognize the importance of action and hard work, and to approach manifestation with a critical eye, understanding its limitations and potential pitfalls.

1. **Clarity and Goal Setting**: Clearly define what you want to manifest. The more specific, the better. Visualize your desired outcome in detail.

2. **Belief and Visualization**: Cultivate a strong belief in the possibility of achieving your goal. Visualize yourself already having what you desire.

3. **Positive Affirmations**: Use positive affirmations to reinforce your beliefs. Speak to yourself as if you already possess what you want.

4. **Taking Inspired Action**: While manifestation involves belief, it also requires action. Take steps aligned with your goals, even if they seem small.

5. **Gratitude**: Focus on gratitude for what you already have. This shifts your energy to abundance and attracts more positive experiences.

6. **Letting Go**: Detach from the outcome. Trust that the universe will provide and let go of control.

At its core, manifestation is the strongest when your belief in the power of the mind is just as strong. Our thoughts and emotions are not just passive observers of our lives. In fact, they are active participants. When we consistently focus on positive thoughts and desires, we create a frequency that attracts similar energies.

If you have negative beliefs about yourself or your ability to achieve your goals, it can hinder your manifestation process. It's important to address and overcome these limiting thoughts. Practice visualization and positive thinking, it's also important to take inspired action toward your goals. Mere thoughts and desires are not enough to manifest your dreams. It is not magic. It takes time and effort to manifest your desires.

If you have unrealistic expectations, you might get discouraged if you don't see immediate results.

Sometimes, external factors beyond your control can influence the outcome of your manifestations. It's important to be flexible and adaptable to unexpected circumstances. If you spend more time focusing on what you don't want than what you do want, it can attract more negative experiences into your life. It's important to maintain a positive focus. It's also important to note that manifestation is not a replacement for hard work, perseverance, and practical action.

When you start practicing manifestation, you'll begin to see changes in your life that you never thought possible. You'll attract more positive experiences, opportunities, and people into your life. You'll feel more confident, happier, and fulfilled. I know it sounds too good to be true, but I promise you, it's real!

During this process of sharing with you all here in this chapter, I reached out to several of my family and friends who either began the practice of manifestation long before I did, or who took the leap of faith during the same time as me, or shortly after, and asked them to share with me some of their personal experiences. Keeping in mind that these are subjective experiences, and the outcomes may have been attributed to various factors, here are some of their findings, experiences, and glimpses into the power of their thoughts:

My friend Liz had always dreamed of working in a specific field in a particular city. She created a vision board, visualized herself in the desired role, and researched companies in the area. While the journey was not without its challenges, she eventually landed a job that perfectly matched her aspirations.

My neighbor Emily was struggling financially immediately after her divorce. Lost in thought and worry, she decided she had nothing to lose when she took the leap of faith and began to focus on abundance and gratitude. Surprisingly, she was approached by an executive in the company where she had been working for a few years. This individual had been observing Emily's work ethic, problem-solving tactics, and leadership skills for a few months. Emily was offered a promotion at work, and she never even applied for the job! It was offered to her unexpectedly and paid significantly more than anticipated.

My friend Luis had been experiencing conflicts in a close relationship. He decided to focus on love, understanding, and forgiveness. Gradually, the communication improved, and the relationship deepened.

My former co-worker Sara was diagnosed with a chronic illness. She focused on healing, visualizing a healthy body, and incorporating positive affirmations. While she continued medical treatment, she experienced a significant improvement in her condition, allowing her body, mind, and soul to feel better as a whole, despite her long road to recovery.

Michael, my good friend's brother, had been searching for the perfect home for months without success. He created a detailed vision of his ideal home, visualized living there, and released his attachment to the outcome. Shortly after, he found a house that perfectly matched his description.

Now, all this time, I have been focusing on sharing the concept of manifestation through the power of positive thoughts and desires. However, this is a two-way road. Not traveling on it for the right reasons or with the understanding of the role, negative manifestations are equally crucial in shaping your life in the direction that it should not be pointing at.

Negative manifestations can be just as powerful, robbing you of self-awareness and personal growth, and keeping you from creating a fulfilling life. By acknowledging and addressing negative thoughts and beliefs, you can gain valuable insights into your self-perception and identify areas for growth. By actively pushing away unwanted experiences or situations, you create space for positive manifestations to enter your life. Nonetheless, there is a silver lining. Negative manifestations can help you clarify your desires and goals by highlighting what you don't want and overcoming negative manifestations can strengthen your resilience and ability to handle challenges.

Use negative manifestations to clearly define what you want to avoid or push away. Allow it to help you focus on the positive. Acknowledge those negative thoughts so you can then shift your focus to positive affirmations and visualizations. Allow yourself to combine negative manifestations with positive actions to create lasting change. Practice self-compassion: Be kind to yourself throughout the process. Talk to a trusted friend, family member, or therapist for guidance and support if you find it difficult to stray from those negative thoughts and practices.

Remember that negative manifestations are not about dwelling on negativity, but more about using them as a tool. It is believed that understanding and harnessing the power of both positive and negative manifestations can lead you to create a life with reduced stress, anxiety, and depression. Lead you to focus on your positive qualities and to believe in yourself and your abilities. Help you to connect with your deeper values and find meaning in your life. When you remain positive and optimistic, you are more likely to attract positive people into your life. Positive manifestation can help you tap into your creative potential and come up with new ideas. It has been linked to improved physical and emotional health.

When I share my thoughts and visions of manifestation with others, most often, I am asked, "So? Is manifestation just like praying"? Manifestation and prayer share fundamental similarities as both involve focusing one's thoughts and intentions to bring about desired outcomes. At their core, both practices focus on the power of belief and the energy of intention. When people pray, they often visualize their desires and express gratitude, which are key components of manifestation. Additionally, both practices can provide comfort, hope, and a sense of control over one's life.

Although it may appear that both manifestation and prayer are somewhat alike, they are as a whole different in their approach and purpose. Prayer is traditionally a spiritual practice. It is the act of faith and surrender. Manifestation is rooted in the belief that people can attract their heartfelt desires through positive thinking and mental visualization, and not seeking a higher power for the occurrence of what they are manifesting.

Some may argue that the similarities between prayer and manifestation make them essentially the same practice. They are both expressed through different cultural and spiritual practices. They each hold the power of intention and belief to bring only positive changes in a person's life. While they both share common elements they each, on their own, are different in practice, and recognizing their differences allows us to understand both in a much deeper understanding and appreciation of both.

It is important to note that positive manifestation is not a magic solution for all of life's problems. However, it can be a powerful tool for creating a more positive and fulfilling life. I've been practicing manifestation for not too long, but I am quickly learning to acknowledge and accept the amazing results. My life has completely transformed, not to its perfection (no one's life will ever be perfect), but certainly, it is where I can experience and live in the moments of my life where I am serving as its conductor.

Ultimately, manifestation is a powerful tool for creating the life you desire. While it may seem unconventional, by understanding the process and applying the steps consistently, you can harness the power of your mind to manifest your dreams into reality. Remember, manifestation is a journey, not a destination. Enjoy the process of self-discovery and growth along the way!

Krystalore Crews

Crews Beyond Limits Consulting, LLC
CEO & People Strategist

https://www.linkedin.com/in/krystalore-crews/
https://www.facebook.com/krystalore
https://www.instagram.com/thecrewscoach/
http://www.krystalorecrews.com/
https://www.facebook.com/groups/crewsbeyondlimits/

Krystalore Crews is a powerhouse in the realm of empowerment, resilience, and holistic well-being. Serving 22 years in the military, she transitioned into entrepreneurship as the CEO of Crews Beyond Limits, a global brand inspiring women to adopt healthier lifestyles. Krystalore, a best-selling author of "Road to Resilience" and creator of the Krystal Clear Life Planner, passionately advocates for dedicating just 34 minutes daily to prioritize health. Her dynamic speaking engagements and global influence position her as a sought-after figure in personal development. With a mission to empower individuals worldwide, Krystalore encourages everyone to join the Crews Beyond Limits community and embark on a journey of empowerment and limitless potential.

Manifesting a Fulfilling Life through the Freedom Formula

By Krystalore Crews

Introduction

Manifestation is a term often surrounded by misconceptions and skepticism. Some view it as mystical or abstract, while others see it as a mere wishful thinking exercise. However, my journey as a Veteran, military spouse, and founder of Crews Beyond Limits has shown me that manifestation is a powerful tool for creating a fulfilling life. It's about setting clear intentions, taking consistent actions, and aligning your thoughts and emotions with your goals. In this chapter, I will delve deeper into my personal journey, explore the concept of emotional intelligence in manifestation, and introduce the Freedom Formula—a framework built on the 5 Cs: Core, Confidence, Consistency, Community, and Celebration. This formula not only helped me navigate the challenges of life but also empowered me to achieve my dreams and help others do the same.

The Journey Begins: Crews Beyond Limits

When I launched Crews Beyond Limits in November 2017, I had a clear vision: To create a global brand and community that would empower women to prioritize their health and well-being. My goal was to live ten steps from the ocean, travel the world hosting transformational workshops and international retreats, and become a best-selling author. I wanted to inspire women to live happier, healthier lives, break generational chains around emotional eating, mental health, and physical well-being, and teach them how to manage stress, have fun, and feel fabulous. However, in 2019, I was diagnosed with cancer, a moment that shook me to my core. It felt like my dreams were slipping away, and I almost gave up on my business and my life.

In a last-ditch effort to find clarity and direction, I attended a business conference. During one of the sessions, we were challenged to create a mind map of our big business ideas. This exercise was transformative. I visualized the global brand I wanted to build, the community I aspired to create, and the impact I desired to have on women's lives. I even wrote down my dream of living ten steps from the ocean in my first self-published book, *Your Krystal Clear Life Planner: A Woman's 90-Day Action Plan to Embrace Chaos and Live a Fulfilling Life!* This exercise helped me reconnect with my vision and set the stage for what was to come.

The Freedom Formula: The 5 Cs

1. Core: Defining Your Values and Vision

At the heart of manifestation lies the concept of the 'Core.' It represents your deepest values, beliefs, and essence of what truly matters to you. Without a clear understanding of your core, it's easy to get lost in the chaos of life. For me, the core of Crews Beyond Limits was about empowering women to take charge of their health and well-being. This clarity helped me stay focused and grounded, even during the most challenging times. As Simon Sinek famously said, "People don't buy what you do; they buy why you do it." Knowing your 'why' is crucial for manifesting your dreams.

2. Confidence: Believing in Your Abilities

Confidence is the cornerstone of successful manifestation. It's about believing in your abilities and having the courage to take bold steps toward your goals. At the conference, I won a contest that changed everything for me. It was a significant confidence booster, reinforcing my belief that I could turn my dreams into reality. I also made my first public Instagram post, declaring my dream of hosting women's wellness retreats worldwide and building a dream team of female Veterans and Military spouses. This public declaration was a powerful act of manifestation, setting a clear intention and sending a message to the universe and myself about my commitment.

Confidence is not just about feeling good about yourself; it's about taking action despite fears and doubts. As Brené Brown says, "You can choose courage or you can choose comfort, but you cannot choose both." Manifestation requires courage—courage to dream big, to put yourself out there, and to take risks. Confidence grows with each step you take and as you see progress, it fuels further action.

3. Consistency: The Daily Commitment

Consistency is the backbone of manifestation. It's about showing up every day, taking small steps toward your goals, and maintaining a disciplined approach. One of the practices that transformed my life was committing to the 34-minute mindset. Every day, I dedicated at least 34 minutes to my health, wellness, and reflection. This daily practice helped me stay aligned with my vision and maintain a clear focus on my goals.

Consistency is about building habits that support your vision. James Clear, the author of *Atomic Habits*, states, "You do not rise to the level of your goals; you fall to the level of your systems." By establishing consistent practices, you create systems that support your goals and make manifestation a natural part of your daily life. Whether it's journaling, meditating, exercising, or planning, consistency builds momentum and keeps you on track.

4. Community: Building a Support Network

Surrounding yourself with a supportive community is essential for manifestation. It's about connecting with like-minded individuals who share your values and goals, and who can offer encouragement, accountability, and support. I've been blessed to build an incredible dream team at Crews Beyond Limits, comprised of 95% female Veterans and Military spouses. Our community has been instrumental in hosting over 10 retreats in three different countries, providing a space for women to heal, grow, and thrive together.

The power of community cannot be overstated. As Jim Rohn famously said, "You are the average of the five people you spend the most time with." Your community influences your thoughts, beliefs, and actions. Being part of a supportive community not only provides practical support but also helps you maintain a positive and growth-oriented mindset. It's a place where you can share your successes and challenges, receive feedback, and find inspiration.

5. Celebration: Recognizing Achievements

Celebration is a vital part of the manifestation process. It's about acknowledging your achievements, no matter how small, and taking time to appreciate the progress you've made. Celebrating your successes reinforces a positive mindset and motivates you to keep going. It's easy to get caught up in the hustle and forget to pause and celebrate how far you've come.

Celebration is not just about big milestones; it's about recognizing the small wins along the way. As Tony Robbins says, "Success without fulfillment is the ultimate failure." Taking time to celebrate keeps you grounded, reminds you of your progress, and helps you stay connected to your 'why.' It also signals to the universe that you are grateful for the opportunities and achievements, which in turn attracts more positivity and success into your life.

Emotional Intelligence and Manifestation

Emotional intelligence (EQ/EI) plays a critical role in manifestation. It's about understanding and managing your emotions, being aware of the emotions of others, and using this awareness to guide your thoughts and actions. As a trauma-informed emotional intelligence coach with over 20 years of experience studying psychology and human behavior, I've seen how powerful the mind is. Our biases, traumas, and experiences can cloud our manifestation glasses, making it difficult to see the possibilities in front of us.

Emotional intelligence helps us navigate these challenges by increasing our self-awareness and emotional regulation. It enables us to recognize limiting beliefs and negative thought patterns that can sabotage our manifestation efforts. By cultivating EQ skills, we can reframe our thoughts, manage stress, and maintain a positive and resilient mindset. This clarity of mind is crucial for setting clear intentions and aligning our actions with our goals.

The Power of Physical and Mental Fitness

Physical and mental fitness are integral to the manifestation process. They provide the energy, focus, and clarity needed to pursue your goals. Exercise and physical activity not only improve your physical health but also boost your mental well-being. They reduce stress, increase energy levels, and enhance mood and cognitive function. This is why I advocate for the 34-minute mindset—dedicating at least 34 minutes a day to activities that nurture your body and mind.

Mental fitness involves practices like meditation, mindfulness, and self-reflection. These practices help calm the mind, reduce stress, and increase clarity and focus. They create a mental space where you can connect with your core values, set clear intentions, and visualize your goals. As Dr. Joe Dispenza, a neuroscientist and author, states, "Where you place your attention is where you place your energy." By focusing your attention on positive and empowering thoughts, you direct your energy towards manifesting your desired outcomes.

Conclusion: The Ripple Effect of Manifestation

Manifestation is not a passive process; it's an active, dynamic journey of growth and self-discovery. By embracing the Freedom Formula and the 34-minute mindset, you can clear the chaos and noise in your life, gain clarity on what sets your soul on fire, and manifest the right things that empower, motivate, and encourage you. This process not only transforms your life but also creates a ripple effect, impacting those around you.

As of the writing of this book, I've hosted over 10 retreats in three different countries and built a remarkable team of female Veterans and Military spouses. This journey has been deeply fulfilling, and it all began with a clear vision and a commitment to the 5 Cs. Manifestation is real, and it's powerful. When your mind is clear, it breeds confidence and opens the door for the universe and/or God to show up with opportunities.

I encourage you to subscribe to the 34-minute mindset, follow the Freedom Formula, and embrace the power of manifestation. Clear your mind, set clear intentions, and take consistent action towards your goals. Remember, you have the power to create the life you desire. Manifestation is not about wishing; it's about believing, acting, and celebrating every step of the journey. Your dreams are within reach—go out and manifest them!

Thank You for Joining The Journey!
Immerse yourself in the art of manifestation.

We are incredibly grateful for your support and enthusiasm for our book! Your engagement is what makes this journey worthwhile.

If these stories resonated with you and you'd like to learn more about the incredible authors featured in this book, please use the links below to connect with them directly. We'd also be so grateful if you could share your thoughts and reviews on the platform where you purchased your copy. Your feedback not only helps others discover the power of manifestation but also helps spread this inspiring message even further!

Cindy Witteman

https://linktr.ee/cindy.witteman
https://drivingsingleparents.org/
https://cfviews.com/
https://cfviews.com/little-give-tv-show-1

Renee Vardouniotis

https://mightyminds.us/
https://www.5thdegree.com/

Sonny Von Cleveland

https://www.tvcfoundation.org/
https://www.heywhiteboy.com/

Norma Cavazos

https://normacavazos.scentsy.us/
https://www.facebook.com/Cavazos4HISD
https://www.facebook.com/profile.php?id=61550591576917&mibex
tid=opq0tG

Krystalore Crews

https://www.krystalorecrews.com/
https://www.facebook.com/groups/crewsbeyondlimits/